FOUNDATIONS FOR

A BETTER KENYA

KENYA BORA

STEPHEN M. MAGU

FOUNDATIONS FOR

A BETTER KENYA

KENYA BORA

Stephen M. Magu
Swahili Village NK
Twenty Three North Ent.
North Kinangop, 20318 KE

This K33P imprint is issued by the independent publisher Kitabu Kipya Kinangop Press, Printing & Publishing, North Kinangop

K33P's registered address is at 5741 Muruaki-Kahuru Scheme, Weru-Kahuru Road, North Kinangop, Kenya, Zip Code 20318

Dedication

Dedicated to Mary Magu

Touched by the politics of a nation, always determined to try

make the best life possible for self, family and other co-citizens

And to the other 55 million Kenyans who toil daily, tirelessly

All who deserve *A Better Kenya*

PREFACE

ඃ෴ඃ෴ඃ෴

This is a blueprint for public policy proposals stemming from the evaluation of the current Kenyan realities. It is the official blueprint and launch of an independent candidacy for the presidential campaign by the author of this proposal. It has been prepared for the public, for the purposes of the forthcoming General Election, to be held as anticipated and planned, on 9th August, 2022, *ceteris paribus.* Through this blueprint, Stephen Magu is most humbled to prepare and to present his candidacy to the people and voters of the Republic of Kenya, for their consideration of those issues that we care deeply about.

In running for election to the office of president, the candidate recognizes and expresses two things. First, that hitherto, our leadership has failed to overcome our ethnic and personality divisions that subsequently make politics about politicians, not about the public policies we Kenyans need. Secondly, an absolute conviction exists, that Kenyans are ready for difference and to elect the fifth president who will be a partner in their goals, hopes and aspirations for better lives for them, their children and for the succeeding generations of Kenyans to come. Success would usher in the 1st, 5th Republic.

The 1st, 5th Republic is proposed because we believe that it is past time to set Kenya onto a new course, to formulate new policies and programs, and to put the country on a new trajectory, a direction that recognizes the many challenges we face. It is a proposed direction that also appreciates the resilience, resources and the determination by Kenyans, to build our country, our efforts to arrive at a better Kenya for ourselves and generations to come, and to bequeath unto them a reflective but progressive and kind, tolerant, better governed, wealthier, well-educated, healthy, economically sound and infrastructurally advanced, all around *A Better Kenya,* Kenya Bora.

The First, Fifth Republic builds on the achievements that Kenya has made over the four presidencies, but proposes to give a new direction to the hopes, plans and aspirations of Kenyans. Although *mwenda pole hajikwai,* the pace of our (lack) of progress is beyond the pale. We may blame our pre-1963 history for some of the ills that we have faced as a nation, but there comes a time to stop blaming others and to begin taking responsibility for our future, our destiny, and to fashion that future with the input of all Kenyans.

The next government has no choice: it has to especially invest in the empowerment of the 37 million (or so) Kenyans who are aged 0–35, and fulfil the long-delayed promise of gender equality, gender equity and access to equal opportunity to the 27+ million women and girls who are now citizens and residents of Kenya, complete with the first female vice-president under 40. This will begin to set us on a better path, but is by no means the only direction of progress we intend to take.

It is important, indeed critical, to clarify that this campaign has no interest in any of the other candidates running for office, except to the extent that their proposed public policies are a concern of each and every Kenyan, and will likely impact us all primarily financially. This is especially true of the seemingly perennial war of words about personalities. If, when and where we differ with their public policy, we will point out the policy differences and nothing more, other than propose *better* alternatives. We will not evaluate any candidate's suitability, or lack thereof, for leadership positions, how long they have been in politics, or whether it is time for others to take up the mantle of leadership. It is up to the Kenyan voters to do so.

We absolutely refuse to engage with any other potential candidates except on the merits of the public policy proposals that they propose. On those, we do welcome robust debate. We welcome civilized, intelligent, informed and non–abrasive debate. Part of this approach is that we do believe that Kenyans deserve *a better politics*, not a politics of persons or personality, but a politics of policies and their effect on Kenyans.

We consider this campaign to be akin to a marathon, or perhaps an FKF game between two major football clubs. No one wins by simply trash-talking their opposition. They do so by competing, and being better at and beating their opponents Our goal is to present you, fellow Kenyan and critical voter, with contending ways to think about our collective destiny, of our desires as a country, of our collective futures, and the path that we take to that future.

This blueprint outlines a programme of action and plans that we know will result in *A Better Kenya – Kenya Bora*. It enunciates our proposed future public policies, adjustments of existing policies and establishes parameters for defining success for the ensuing administration. It proposes a several programs and plans and revisions of current public policies, designed to build sustainable jobs and create wealth, arrive at a more just society, and reanimate Kenyans' pride to proclaim again that *najivunia* rather than *najihurumia* or *naumia kuwa Mkenya*.

We fashion this blueprint based on a number of key issues of interest and importance to Kenyans. We beginning with the obvious: government, governance and the rule of law, leadership, devolved county and local government working in tandem to improve the lives of Kenyans, and improving the economy, trade and agriculture, some of which are connected and change in tandem (as they should).

Other areas of new proposals in public policy include food security, the place of women and more broadly gender and equity, what critical infrastructure the country has and needs, the most important area perhaps of all, healthcare, life expectancy and wellness, education and pupils' educational outcomes, youth future and human resources, research, development, technology and innovation; public service, human security and insecurity; foreign policy; environment, stewardship and climate change; society, culture and our socio-cultural traditions.

This blueprint also outlines other important issues that do not neatly fall under any of these specific categories. We also acknowledge that we are not an exclusive source of (good) ideas, and therefore, we welcome robust discussion and engagement, so that we can vet these ideas, discard impractical ones and incorporate new, better ideas.

To reiterate: we do *want* to only engage in ideas, not in personalities. Throughout this campaign, in all our platforms, we are dedicated to avoid the usual 'Kenyan politics' of people this and people that. Ideas and policy proposals, we believe, are what will move this country to better outcomes, better economy, better government, and a better society come August

9th, 2022. It is time, and it is half past necessary, for all of us, and our fellow Kenyans, to choose *A Better Kenya*.

North Kinangop, Kenya   Stephen M. Magu

ACKNOWLEDGMENTS

ೞೞೞೞೞೞ

This short volume is a result of many conversations with a large variety of Kenyans, who may not always have known that the conversations they entered into with a passenger on their motor-bike, in their Uber or Bolt ride-share, in conversations with a nondescript passenger in a *Matatu*, a light-hearted humor with a pharmacist or a small-business owner, would contribute to the impetus for a change in how politics is done in Kenya. Many conversations with my nephew, James, and his cousins, were very illuminating in helping think through public policy and what we might do different, *better*, as a nation. The privilege of travel to other countries has, and continues to allow me to gain insight into how one can achieve goals such as trains running on time and efficiently, or some of the changes that are necessary to bring about sustainable changes. Practical realities, such as the inability of older Kenyans to obtain health insurance and having little by way of income to support themselves or pay for hospital costs and medications absent a universal health cover, resorting to Harambees, were also especially informative and influential in this attempt to propose pathways to *A Better Kenya.*

Contents

Raison d'être: Why President, Why Movement?

ೞೞೞೞೞೞ

How much time and effort do our current leaders, especially those seeking the presidency during the 2022 General Election, spend on discussing their comprehensive plans for why they are running for office? We hear about political movements: OKA, UDA, Mount Kenya – and a myriad of political parties that are started, joined, left, discarded, newly reconstructed and are used as vehicles for individuals to be elected to parliament, Senate, Governors, MCAs, Women's Rep and the presidency. These are all good and proper, except that the parties are not vastly different when we boil them down to essentials.

There are two self-evident truths that most of the political class leave out when they discuss your role as a citizen. First, that coalitions are necessary (mostly, because the parties are regional and or ethnic and no one group has more than 22 percent of the vote, even if the community voted to a man; no one group can rule Kenya without the others).

Secondly, you, as a citizen, rarely feature in these discussions about why this coalition, or that coalition, or this leader or that, is better for your overall welfare, than that other leader, or their party. There is little regard to the benefit that you, as a citizen, accrues upon specific leaders being elected and assuming office, since implicitly, the election it is unlikely to affect your life significantly unless you are a relative of those in power.

Now, although campaign season is not officially ongoing, you often hear the most basic discussion of "hustler narratives" or "top-down" economy, and which of the models is better than the other. There are many things these 'policies' – we do assume that they are policies they intend to implement once they win the presidency – that they do not say to you.

There is especially very scant discussion of the next steps of the economic models: for example, what is 'top-down' models and isn't this what Kenya has done for the past 60 years? In its most basic form, 'top-down' is 'trickle-down' and while it may have worked in the US, it is not clear how in a farming nation, you have a top-down economic model unless you want to do the anti-Mugabe in Zimbabwe (consolidate farms and perhaps have most people working on them). Reminds one of colonial Kenya, and that is not a good experience.

The second policy proposal for an economic model does not tell us the following: 'what comes after all youth, vijanas (remember, 37 million under-35) and *Mama Mboga* each have a small business? How do we scale up to the next thing, or are we to believe that sole proprietorships might lead us to LMIC and other statuses we have aspired to, as part of our 2030 vision and Agenda 2063? But these are more loftier debates that lend themselves to more intellect than practice at this point.

No matter who gets elected on 9th August 2022, we the Kenyan citizens can be certain that we face most of the same conditions that we will be facing on the *8th* of August, but our decisions will influence the future directions. On 10th of August, the day after the General Election, we still will:

❑ Continue to pay more across education: for school tuition, uniforms, the 'non-existent' tuition, printing pictures of

CBC kids 'on vacation with their family swimming in a lake' (and they live in Mandera), among other expenses

- [ ] Pay 16% VAT on all products even as the average income continues to stagnate and purchasing power erodes, thus gradually making everything expensive (more money buys less stuff, but not quite Zimbabwe-style)
- [ ] Continue to experience hunger and drought especially in some areas of the country, while those in power continue to fuel chase vehicles – to chase you from the road
- [ ] Experience corruption on a day to day basis, in the matatus you ride in, if you try to get service, or a child into the uniform services, or your child into this or that school
- [ ] Suffer intermittent electrical blackouts despite the huge potential for solar power grids independent of the Kenya Power and Lighting Candles and its authorizing legislation
- [ ] Be unable to purchase health insurance (besides NHIF) if a person is over 65 years of age (these are our parents,
- [ ] Confront long, unending lines at hospitals and woe unto you if you should be admitted, find that your NHIF card will not pay your entire bill and family doesn't have the million plus shillings that is your medical bill: you will be detained in hospital until you clear it
- [ ] See one's children unable to join some secondary school or tertiary institution because they 'failed' – 90 percent of all Kenyan students 'fail' by this measure, an undeniably unacceptable idea, unless we want to suggest we are an academically 'failing' nation
- [ ] Continue to experience poverty while their MPs and other elected officials pay little tax, get car grants and get paid more than 10X the annual average income of the citizen
- [ ] Experience ever high costs of transportation, fuel and cost of essential goods: the more you work, the poorer you get

☐ Face other every-day indignities that government can and should alleviate, including disrespect getting detained.

It is not far-fetched to impute the reasons for individuals' practice of giving up their liberties to enter into government with others anywhere and everywhere. The reasons therefore are clear and mostly invariant. To quote and paraphrase one of the best and most enduring constitutions around the world, who incidentally also suffered the vagaries of control by the self-same rulers, i.e., the British, by throwing off the yoke of British expression – or more accurately, tyranny – then forming a *Republic*, the people of Kenya aimed to establish a version of 'justice, tranquility, common defense' and 'promote the general welfare' of Kenyans.

Kenya describes itself as a *Republic.* Deriving from the Latin 'res publica,' the concept is generally translated to mean a 'public affair' and in the common usage, implies a self-governing entity. If one goes deeper into consensus government, then republic is closer to a democracy. It is also defined as 'commonwealth' to denote a, or the, body politic. What is most important is that as a Republic, sovereign power resides in us, the citizens, and in exercise these, we *do* establish government.

Government is a vehicle, a facilitator, created to 'promote the general welfare' common to and desired by all Kenyans. But it quite often needs ongoing reminders that it serves at the behest of the people, not the other way. Citizens then emplace strategies, structures and parties, hence this *Movement for a Better Kenya*, where the citizens' general welfare is promoted. This has not been the case for the most part.

As often as government has protected, some of the very worst excesses have been committed by the same. Government has oppressed, rather than facilitated the pursuit of lives free of 'most troubles.' To restore the proper purpose of government and to achieve the purposes for which government is crafted, our central to our promise to our fellow citizens, our contract with Kenya is to ensure that government works for the people. The people do *not* work for government (they may have jobs).

The *angst* that exists and drives this movement for *A Better Kenya* stems from the absolute conviction that 'a better Kenya is possible.' Kenyans should, and have the right to expect better, to have high standards of living, education, jobs, security, prosperity and generally, living fulfilling lives. And mostly, for the government to stay out of their business, and when public policy is made, for such policy to be pro-parents, not government.

Anyone who desires to live "On the Hill," which is the term this treatise uses to refer to Kenya's State House, either has the spirit of a servant leader, or a desire for near-unconstrained power. Power can help them improve the lives of fellow citizens, and if they are private entrepreneurs, it can also help them improve their own.

To wake up each day and look down the hill, and see, or even imagine Kibera, ought to remind State House's occupant(s) of the minimum level of responsibility they have, and the power that comes with their office, to *make the lives of their fellow citizens better, each day.* Anyone who sees Kibera in the morning ought to not be able to sleep, or do everything so that by evening they can credibly and honestly say, "I have given it my best." It is not our assessment that this has been done.

A president, the president of Kenya, is clothed in immense power, power of persuasion, leadership and of being an exemplar. Although the president must be constrained by the Constitution, the Laws of Kenya, some elements of precedence and the other co-equal branches of government, the leadership they can propose and produce can change the trajectory of a country and a people. Has Kenya been the best that it can be, to its citizens? It is not clear that it has.

What vision have the four preceding Kenyan presidents given and have they been able to execute the vision? Have our leaders shown us that we can build a better Kenya or helped build the said better Kenya? Do we as a country provide our youth with full employment? Is our education system good, and how does it stack up against the rest of the world? How about health care? How should we adjudge a health insurance system that makes it near impossible to obtain health insurance for older adults over 65 years of age, who are at the point of diminishing health and ability?

Are we ensuring that we have regard for other human beings and especially our fellow Kenyans? What about the environment? Did we ditch the paper bags, only to clog the same spaces with the ubiquitous masks? How are we (if we are) providing for the indigent, infirm, elders, orphans, street children and needy? Do we have a *working* policy for them? Considering that we are an agrarian state and our economy is heavily dependent on the same, how can we eliminate perennial droughts and resource conflicts?

Has our past leadership excelled in doing the things that we need done, in order to get to whatever promised lands, the proposed futures that we have endeavored to reach? We think not. Our leadership has achieved some of the said goals, but Kenya is not exactly a roaring success perhaps in anything but long distance races. 60 years after liberation, it is time for us to change our direction and be *better* Kenyans in a *better* Kenya.

Besides this being a presidential campaign, this is also a long-term movement. *A Movement for a Better Kenya*. The country will not just magically improve whatever the outcomes of the 2022 general election will be. Thus, it is a movement whose objectives include seeing to it that some of these obvious, necessary and even urgent proposals are implemented by our, or the succeeding government. Whoever wins in 2022, kids still need IDs, Free education still needs to happen. The CBC needs to be revised, irrespective of what the abrasive and rather incredulous policy-maker at the helm of the education system today alleges.

This is thus more than just a political campaign. It is conceived more as a movement, a contract between we the citizens, the governed, and those entrusted with the solemn obligation to do those things that improve the lives of Kenyans, for and on behalf of the said Kenyans, and for their benefit, the Republic, here, now and in future.

It is a contract that seeks to holds the elected officials to account, to contribute to public policy-making, to improve the overall individual and general conditions before, during and especially after the election. This is not a movement that will go anywhere; in fact, it will hold all elected officials accountable in order to make Kenyans lives much, much better.

We could spend time contemplating the different individuals who have led the country, but that would be more of the same, and the goal of this short treatise is to propose a different path for a country, now approaching 60 years of republic, and still going through some of the same challenges it did the day it became independent. This short treatise is concerned with the policies, some from the past (for they illustrate the present and future) and their deficiency.

This proposal, this contract with fellow Kenyans is a blueprint for '*A Better Kenya*,' '*Kenya Bora*.' It is built around the major, even critical issues that Kenyan (citizens or their elected representatives) should ask themselves every day this

Republic exists. They include the score-card of how Kenya has stacked up with respect to the goals that it set out, and as it attempts to fulfil its most sacred responsibilities to the Kenyan citizens. There are also questions regarding the country's important roles and obligations to regional and global publics, considering how the world is interconnected.

Introduction

ଔଽ୦ଔଽ୦ଔଽ୦

As a Kenyan citizen, one has an interest in living a life that is not, in the words of an ancient philosopher, too much beset by troubles. Most voting Kenyan citizens, *the sovereign,* default to choosing leaders who will make the decisions that are necessary for the *welfare* of the *body politic.* We have implicit faith, especially after the experiences with the colonial government, that they will act in the best interests of the Kenyan people, especially considering that one has no liberty to be stateless.

Any group of people comes together in union, because in one way or another, together is generally considered 'better' than apart. Whether together is a good thing for all is a different discussion, as is the question of 'consent.' Part of the preamble to Kenya's 2010 Constitution reads as follows: "*exercising* our sovereign and inalienable right to determine the form of governance of our country and having participated fully in the making of this Constitution..."[1] Kenyans contributed to drafting, passing, voting and ultimately, cheering for and upon promulgation of the new constitution, but whether or not they gave consent to be in Kenya, to be Kenyans, in the first place, is another matter.

Membership to Kenya impose both responsibilities as well as privileges. As taxpayers (even the zero-filers and those exempt due to age still pay tax – VAT), there are those expectations that citizens have of their government, including things that simply should work better, decisions and policies that improve our lives. These may include such lofty ideals as explicated in, for example, the US Declaration of Independence, that government is instituted so as to provide conditions favoring "Life, Liberty and the pursuit of Happiness" people have and exercise the "Right [...] to alter or to abolish it, and to institute new Government."[2]

Change in government, in who rules, is almost central, if not part, of the democratic process, and Kenya is a democratic republic. We propose not some radical and far-reaching changing of government; rather, to institute a government that pursues a different path so as to achieve things we began deliberating in 1963 at independence. We can't say that we have eradicated 'poverty, ignorance and disease.'[3] We do not have clean water, universal education (it is peppered with so many different fees). We do not have gender equality. We have not quite bonded as one nation; we occasionally fight. We have not found a way to eradicate nepotism, even though we know that the best person for the job should get it. We are far, far from the promised land our founders envisioned and fought for.

We believe that accomplishing these goals is within reach, and that they can be accomplished in our lifetime. As one community so eloquently notes, 'being promised something is not the same as being given the same thing, and even when it is in the mouth, it can be taken away.' True, we have progressed, and embraced a lot of technology and modernity, so that we *know* how to change and lead in such areas as Mobile Money. That previous governments were riven by nepotism, ineffectiveness, autocracy and other ills is well chronicled, but if we spend time looking back, we will fail to see all the opportunities and challenges that lie ahead of us.

That said, it is necessary to consider a different path, one that will lead to the achievement of that which looks to be impossible, or has been in the past 60 years or so. Of right and out of the contract that government makes with its citizens, we do have expectations *of* government and in exchange for our membership in the collective that is Kenya. Among these, we know that Kenyans want, and expect:

- ☐ Better leadership, better ideas and opportunities to build better futures for themselves and their children
- ☐ Better public policy and decision-making, in order to more carefully and increasingly favor, even leverage opportunity, not measly handouts (ok, they probably do want handouts too, but perhaps only because of the levels of need)
- ☐ Better politics that is not about money, at least not the Kshs. 100 they give. As Kipipiri once showed it is possible to get elected purely on the basis of good ideas
- ☐ Co-government between citizens and corruption-free leaders and officials, and to know they can conduct business with government without having to pay extra 'taxes' for things that ought to be free
- ☐ Political parties that stand for something so that they don't fall for anything; parties that have philosophies which define them and that are distinguishable from each other rather than simply being defined by the leader's name
- ☐ Policies, not just political parties or personalities are the driver for this campaign and Kenya's leadership should consider a higher level of discourse as they serve Kenya.

In partnership with Kenya and Kenyans, we believe that these we can achieve, and these are what we seek to provide. An election that happens only once every five years confers both opportunity and responsibility, and we cannot always blame the leaders when we choose them, particularly when we have opportunities. We must appreciate and internalize the Einsteinian saying so prodigiously repeated by Obama, that "insanity [as] doing the same thing over and over and expecting different results."[4] But more significantly, we must build a better nation.

Government, Governance and the Rule of Law

Although the subject of corruption and why we do not seem to have any capacity to deal with it is tackled elsewhere, it deserves advance mention. Nothing has impacted Kenyans' well-being more than corruption, and yet we seem unable to stop it. Even though corruption is not just a Kenyan problem, we have always ranked near the bottom of World Bank Governance Indicators and Transparency International Corruptions Perceptions Index. There is nothing worse that citizens having little to no trust in government, as COVID-19 vaccine hesitancy has shown.

It is imperative, that we constitute a government that is going to be a partner in solving the challenges that Kenyans face. There is ample evidence that Kenyans can, and *want* good government and governance. One wonders where the disconnect is. Perhaps we should mandate that public officials educate their children in Kenya and that they go to the same hospitals that we do, that they give up their police escort and four-wheel drive cars, so that they know what cattle tracks are. Perhaps we should make them pay taxes and take away the car and house grants, or make them available to all Kenyans on the principle of equality. But since none of these will happen, it is on us Kenyans, to elect leaders with better policies.

Regarding graft and the corruption that pervades society today, we absolutely must do more than put this on God. Today, we pray about corruption and craft institutions that are incapable, or that are designed with so many weaknesses and failure points, that we do see it is simply an attempt to *look like we are doing something,* not actually doing anything. We prosecute literally no one, and when we do, it is the fish-eggs, not even the small fish. Over 22 years of having anti-corruption agencies, none of them has been effective by even the most generous measures. It is not clear that it is impossible to eradicate the vice.

We need good government. Good government, and governance, begin with the kind of leaders we elect. It is often said that a people get the kinds of leaders they deserve. We cannot, should not believe that somehow, we are the cursed of East Africa, that we are destined to be one of the most corrupt nations in the region. With every instance, every report, every act, every action, we almost validate the proposition arising mostly from the west, that we are unable to govern ourselves. If only to prove others wrong (but also, to really vastly and drastically improve the lives of Kenyans), we have to do better. We have to believe in, and to commit to building *A Better Kenya.*

Chapter 1: Leadership and Governance: 1963 to Present

1. What is the character of leadership in Kenya and has it helped the country to progress?
2. Do Kenyan leaders measure up to the greatest leaders and ideals that Kenyans value (and what are those)?
3. What role do Kenyans play in the development of the leaders that we have in Kenya today?
4. How can we improve Kenyan leadership, to escape the 'bandit nation mentality' that pervades us?

Introduction

Has Kenya experienced good leadership in its near six decades of independence? It is probably important to consider what constitutes 'good leadership.' In the context of nations, and specifically, to Africa, good leadership might be as simple as avoiding the perennial wars that appear to be in Africa's DNA. Good leadership can be seen as the antithesis of bad leadership.

It is decidedly certain that Kenya has been ruled more productively than Somalia, or Ethiopia, or D. R. Congo. But that does not mean that Kenya has had good leadership. Good leadership entails more than simply avoiding the worst possible outcomes. Yes, Kenya has generally avoided all-out conflict, but who can forget 1992, 1997 and 2007, election periods that saw the worst in all of us?

Successive Kenyan leadership has run the gamut of violating citizens' rights, enduring corruption, propagating conflict during election periods, muzzling freedoms of expression, misusing public resources, extra-judicially killing citizens and disappearing others. They have presided over overtaxing citizens without commensurate services provided, committing wholesale massacres (e.g., the Wagalla Massacre), facilitating both institutional and petty corruption, deceiving its citizens, failing to secure the nation against foreign threats such as the Al Shabaab.

They have allowed environmental degradation, poaching and illicit sale of wildlife products, overfishing, sale of sketchy food products and a host of other issues. Does this necessarily make Kenya's leadership history 'less than'? Not necessarily. In countries including the leading democracies around the world, crime, corruption, murders and occasionally, government-sanctioned massacres have occurred. Good leadership cannot stop every possible evil man can conjure, but purposely bad leadership actively facilitates these vices. Think the Khmer Rouge, or closer home, of Idi Amin.

Good leadership conducts itself in the public interest, and the public interest is not merely elites' interests. African countries such as Senegal, Gambia and Botswana long stood as beacons of stability and democracy. One of the most important elements of this enviable stamp of approval was good leadership. Good leadership is neither ordained, nor lifelong.

At minimum, it improves the lives and conditions of citizens of a country, which can be measured through such indices as life expectancy, level of education, income levels, quality of life, access to resources, labor, government services, even ability to petition government. These are some of the areas in which the Kenyan government has failed its citizens. They are neither exhaustive, nor have they been demonstrably remedied.

Policymaking in Kenya is especially poor, murky and rarely involves citizens in the form of hearings and expert testimony. We educate all these citizens and place them in positions where they will implement policy, but do not seek their input as to the possible benefits and harms of policies. In a highly patriarchal system, it appears that Kenyan citizens' role in their government is restricted to only electing their representatives, who then make policy not necessarily in the interest of their constituents, but in their own interest. One only has to look at how quickly legislation regarding MPs pay, sitting allowances, travel and other benefits, tax exemptions, car grants and housing grants and facilities passes, while other key pieces of legislation that could actually help citizens, is near non-existent.

National Government policies are equally befuddling, and many examples of this are clear. They include recent examples such as mandating vaccination for all citizens even though at the time, there were only about million available shots, thus requiring citizens to have something that only government could provide but was not *and* requiring vaccination was befuddling. In education, the overall year has effectively shortened to about 6 months, and each school term is now about two months in length. Government policy required, expected that parents pay the same amounts of money, even though most are farmers.

What is most interesting is that the taxpayers who pay the policymaker are met with near-rude responses about not being sufficiently invested in their children's education, shirking their responsibilities, and all manner of negligence. One cannot help but wonder if there could be a policy that commands crops to grow in half the time. At the same time, the government was in the middle of implementing all kinds of problematic new curriculum that requires significant investment in technology, and parents' input, without the said investments. The policy response is often, "deal with it."

Servant Leadership by Good Capitalists?
Kenya prides itself as a democratic capitalist nation. The first is peculiar, the second is accurate, but perhaps the worst form of capitalism. Leadership in Kenya appears to only have one objective: get in office and find ways to 'reap the benefits of office' which include access to government contracts and tenders, increasing one's salary, benefits and tax-free car grants, sitting allowances to do essentially nothing, and travel by elected officials on taxpayer dime to foreign countries for such preposterous purposes as to study how oranges are grown in Israel, as though they would then return to Kenya and become desert orange farmers.

The issue of Kenya's leadership deficits is one of ideology, investment and ideals. Good leadership requires investment in the idea of a nation, belief that Kenya is a united nation, and that Kenya is a collective, which surpasses the individual, even though it is a collection of individuals. Some of the elements of poor leadership are obvious, but facilitated by top-to-bottom attitudes towards leadership.

The police officer who takes Kshs. 100 (or whatever the amount) from a drunk driver, or some driver of an unroadworthy vehicle, or an overloaded Matatu) and lets the vehicle pass risks having his own family killed by a drunk driver or in accidents with mechanically unsound vehicles. Up the chain, a corrupt individual who grabs public land (especially road reserves) and sells to different individuals, hopes for the best, but as Kenya constructs roads, hundreds of millions have been lost as property is demolished or abandoned.

The greatest risk to Kenya's leadership is the self-serving nature of some who enter into public office. No one candidate, or leader, has seemed to believe in a Kenya that is fair and just, where everyone has an equal chance of making it in life, and where public office does not mean robbing the public, legally or otherwise. The highest ideal of leadership in Kenya seems to be 'how much can I grab, steal, or benefit from being in office?' This leads to the massive amounts of money spent in campaigns, but also, the near universal accusation of anyone who has held significant public office of corruption.

Nothing in this suggests that leaders should not be well-paid for their work, to the extent that it also uplifts citizens. The phrase that 'rising tides lift all boats' is true, but again, we harken back to *Animal Farm's* 'all animals are equal, but some are more equal than others.' Nothing could be more true of Kenya. Most leaders seem to be more Kenyan than the rest of Kenyans, and it is not clear that this doesn't even violate the Constitution.

For some of our citizens who enter public office, we also see the overnight riches, borne of no-bid contracts awarded to companies that were only registered two days before a tender is available. Most subsequent public hearings have the same outcome: no one knows anything, people saw 'a vision' and offered some ministry or other services or goods and it happened to have the need and therefore purchased overpriced, Kshs. 100,000 wheel barrows and such. And despite Kenya having one of the most robust electronic registration systems for cell-phones, which are used to register companies through E-Citizen accounts, the certificates of registration of companies cannot be found, neither can their owners, yet the company was awarded almost US$2 million no–bid contract.

Past Kenyan leadership, their actions and leaders themselves have done everything to undermine faith in government, a government they serve. Faith in government is like an egg. Once you break it, you can try to scoop it up and tape it back together, but that is a leaky egg that is permanently destroyed. Our leaders do not appear to have any investment in anything other than themselves. This is the worst possible model of leadership.

It creates a coercive, not consensual state. And since nothing happens to the leaders who have stolen from Kenyans, what is there to stop the corruption? Consider how many convictions have (not) been completed by Kenyan courts, even against the petty corruption that is openly conducted – like the stuff you witness any time you are in a Matatu and see that Kshs. 50 note handed over by the driver. Perhaps it is a challenge to fry bigger fish, but the small ones? Tragically, the cycle seems to repeat: the next group that come into office follow the same path, with newer ideas of how to fleece the public. Some suggest that even devolution became devolution of corruption so that 'more people eat.' Politics and government become a game of musical chairs by individuals dubiously elected, who, even though they deny it vehemently, more often than not buy votes.

A careful study of most candidates for office suggests that they use a most cunning combination of an appeal to the public by promising to implement their almost-vision for Kenya. It is achieved mostly through their candidacies once elected into office. But when the elections are over, citizens rarely see these officials until close to the next election, at least in the context of policy discussion and formulation. Even though they couch development in terms of "we", leaders appear to be in a race for personal glorification and enrichment.

The existing public institutions are frequently used as election financing coffers, with an eye to the future of contracts and tenderpreneurship. Courts are used to endlessly drag matters so that no conclusion is arrived at even when allegations of corruption and other nefarious actions have been referred to the judicial system, *a la* '45. It is almost as though Kenya has become a bandit nation, with justice for the most money, and the public screwed by endless stalling and appeals.

Our leaders do not have a grand scheme, at least one that they have publicly and clearly articulated, i.e., a vision for the country, for the future. Actually, they do. The 'grand scheme', the goal of their very 'service' is to self. They are the 'highest ideal', but it is one that does not track with what Kenya should be. If Kenya is not an oligarchy, there is probably no other country that could attract that label. It is a country of the few, for the few, by the few, and everyone else is essentially – SOL. These inequities have led to the peculiar conditions where leaders and the wealthy essentially live in 'prison.' Prison, since the economic inequities and their relative luxury leave them vulnerable to robbery. It has led to the erection of high walls with broken glass, electric fences and the hiring of security guards, which is clearly no way to live if you are that wealthy.

Kenya has far too many scandals that are in the public domain, some of which have robbed Kenya of wealth up to 20 percent of the economy, such as the Goldenberg saga. It is incomprehensible that individuals who are outside of government and who profess no 'hacker collective' types of skills (and are in fact 'office assistants'), are able to divert hundreds of millions of shillings through government computers into personal bank accounts without triggering a five-alarm level of caution.

It follows then, that, unless those in charge want to facilitate siphoning of such funds, they would have the most robust IT safeguards available anywhere. But that would make it too difficult to get around them, in case you had need to. Again, it appears that the key question that is asked in creating such systems is: '(how) can we get around the safeguards instituted by the system?' Systems seem to be built with conscious flaws, so that they can be breached, rather than the opposite as you may expect: un-hackable. And this does not even account for that especially uniquely Kenyan practice of 'tenderpreneurship.'

Countries and leaders can be beacons, and embodiment of good leadership, setting a country onto a less-corruptible path. Consider Singapore. Singapore's split from Malaysia in 1965, perhaps the quickest 'states' divorce' in the history of nations, was intended to punish Singapore which disfavored the special place of Malays in the Malaysian federation. Singapore (and Malaysia's) economic conditions in 1965 mirrored then-Kenya.

Today, Singapore is one of the most affluent nations on the planet. Granted, it is a relatively small nation with $^1/_9$ of Kenya's population and a mere 472.3 km^2 but no one doubts that Lee Kuan Yew was one of the most influential leaders in Singapore, the greater East Asia and in the Global South. LKY did not preside over a democratic nation, but the outcomes of the Singaporean experiment are there to be seen: vision is often more important than ineffectual institutions. Kenya is blessed with both: lack of leadership and ineffectual institutions.

Good, honest leadership ought to be truthful with Kenyans, and acknowledge realities of a heterogeneous nation. But we are a nation, and we find ourselves bound by the same borders, constitution, leaders, institutions and practices. Therefore, we are in this together, and need to act like we know and believe it. The pursuit of the presidency is one of the most divisive periods in the country's 60 year history.

Honest leaders should, and have the responsibility to educate Kenyans that no one community can win the presidency without the others, and so it is necessary to create coalitions that do not seek to benefit one group or community over another, creating future incentive for excluded groups to clamor for their own piece of the pie. But we should probably also make the presidency less of a zero-sum game, so that conflict *do not* result from most elections.

Ideological Leadership Agenda: non!
Leadership is also about principles. These are principles that presumably guide an individual, their conduct, their desire to serve their fellow mankind, essential compass, a north star hopefully of born of righteous purpose. Can one easily identify such a compass in their own lives, even before they enter into leadership? And can they subsequently avoid the time-honored precept that holds that 'absolute power corrupts absolutely'? Perhaps they can, and do, and it might be the case that Kenya is too difficult a country to administer, and that the righteous purpose for which candidates seek elective office cannot be fulfilled in such a divided society as Kenya.

Whether one appeals to religion and the most powerful commandments, e.g., love being the greatest of them all (commandments), or to the so-called 'Golden Rule,' or the more African concept of 'ubuntu,' there is sufficient spiritual guidance as to how we should treat our fellow man. But what do leaders wake up each day planning to do? Are they driven by an urge to solve the most pressing issues in their society?

This candidate has a simple and somewhat combined mantra-vision: do no harm, *and* dedicate each day to 'improving the human condition.' It is not always clear that one is improving the human condition by working a regular job, but leadership is vision, it is important and necessary to dedicate oneself to reaching the highest and noblest ideals of not just their own achievement, but also of their fellow mankind. To rise to a position of leadership in Kenya ought to require that a leader wakes up each morning dedicated to doing everything they can to build a better world for *all* Kenyans.

It is not possible to see Kibera from State House – or any of the other low-income housing estates (or slums) that house more than half of Nairobi's 3 million residents. It is also likely that people who sleep in State House have one of those sleep number beds contouring to their tired bodies after all that work, making speeches, cavorting with diplomats, dispensing cash to all and sundry and riding motorcades all day.

They must not know, or (have to) see, their fellow citizens only 5 km away from the grand residence first built by the British, as they go through each day of their lives, living in shanties over flowing, raw sewage, wondering but not able to do anything about potential health risks, personal safety, poor environmental hygiene and living conditions, but raising kids and hoping that their offspring will be better off than they are.

Or, they do not care, and just see *votes.*

It is necessary for us, as Kenyans, to decide that the *status quo* is unacceptable. We have to reject the current reality suggesting that we are unable, or perhaps unwilling, to provide clean drinking water, quality healthcare and coverage especially for our elderly and inform (while ironically promoting the proposition of having more kids by providing free maternity and reproductive health services), a high quality, modern, utilitarian and completely free education, and therewith, a fair shot at life that is not predicated on working in agriculture for eternity.

We have to; we must articulate a different vision of the country we all share, call home and doubtlessly, love. We must ask and demand that we do not live in a society where some live in bungalows and others in shanties. Our vision for Kenya is a fair, just, equitable, egalitarian society. We envision a society that is governed by the rule of law, good governance, economic development, individual freedoms, and informed by the values of ubuntu and the care for our fellow citizens.

No, we do not need to create a socialist nation, just one that gives every citizen an equal chance, and one whose policies are not tilted to always benefit the haves. We should aim to live in a modicum of a Platonic Kallipollis in government, but one in which every child has an equal, fair chance at an education that will not be stopped by a 'failing' grade over whether they know that spiders are arachnids, or kept out of a job because they don't know 'the right people' or have money to pay up the 'facilitation fee' (or bribe), or be denied by a long life by the pollution in the environment they live in. We must articulate a vision for a better, kinder, gentler Kenya.

Leaders often articulate their ideas in written form, either defending them before, during or after their time in office. It is exceedingly rare to see Kenyan, and more broadly, African leaders (besides Nkrumah, Nyerere and a few others) write anything but biographies. Whereas some of the books do explain the life trajectory of the individual, that is less interesting unless it gives us insight into the decisions they have made.

On the other hand, a lot of decisions are haphazard, *ad hoc*, rarely informed by public discourse, and in retrospect, absolutely terrible. Is this what our leaders are afraid of, that in time, they will be judged harshly by history? They do not need to worry. The millions of children living in poverty, having less than enough to eat, dropping out of school, being subject to GBV because "it is our African traditions" are being judged and pronounced guilty of abdicating their major responsibility to the citizens of Kenya, even as they continue get paid.

Kenyans' Roles

Some of the poor leadership Kenya experiences is attributable to Kenyans themselves, and to our belief in 'eating.' Not just food; campaign money that seems to become available nearer the elections. Every five years, during the national elections, candidates for office traverse the country, presumably sharing their vision for the nation they seek to lead and of the offices that they aim to ascend into and hopefully, serve Kenyans.

But we really know that as Kenyans, all the crying in all of Africa might not interest us in any policy proposals as much as the money that leaders dish out. *Some live for that moment, that money.* Surreptitiously, but just as equally, fairly openly, the candidates distribute money to the assembled future supporters and voters (or opportunists), with amounts ranging from Kshs. 100 to no more than Kshs. 500 for the most generous, depending. Such vote-buying is often described as 'drinking soda' or 'buying a *leso.*' One surmises that there is a fair discussion of the need for sodas especially during those hot days, but corruption and vote-buying by any other name is just vote-buying.

Some Kenyans actively seek out the opportunity to obtain such pre-election goodies, figuring that the only time – besides in Harambees and other public functions – where they will have an opportunity to benefit from the political system – is before elections. This is short-sightedness, the pursuit of short term gains in favor of potential policy changes that would be far more financially valuable and long-term.

Tragically hilariously, Kenyans argue that it is *their* time to 'eat' from any candidate who seeks their vote, and that if the offer is there, no one really could possibly turn down good money. After all, it is possible to 'eat' and still vote for the candidate of one's choice, assuming that the latter is actually based on a study of the candidate's policy positions.

But just like the corrupt police officer allows a drunk driver to drive on with no regard to the possible negative outcomes like an accident, citizens who 'sell' their vote without demanding those kinds of changes that improve their well-being are settling for the least possible benefit. It is unbelievably self-defeating. Then again, people regularly vote against their interests, and Kenyans have shown this to be the case.

Take two hypothetical citizens and future voters. One decides to take the money and ends up, through the campaign season, with Kshs. 1,000 (the other wants the future elected official, say a Member of Parliament, to sponsor lawmaking that makes tuition free). Kshs. 1,000 is 'some' amount of money but taking that amount, then voting to send an MP to parliament, an MP who will earn at least 1,000 times the same amount they gave to the constituent (estimating a salary, allowances and grants at near Kshs. 1.x million a month) for *five* years, is a terrible outcome.

On the other hand, if the MP actually sponsored legislation to make education free, and this said constituent had a child about to enter secondary school, even estimating Kshs. 50,000 a year for 4 years, the benefit would be 200 times the Kshs. 1,000 the second constituent would forego. This is absolutely a better outcome, but short-term gains (and alcohol) might drive one to favor the lesser, instantaneous amount.

Good leaders and citizens who are committed to a better future will want to educate themselves and others, that foregoing Kshs. 1,000 temporary benefit in favor of better legislation is ultimately a more productive path to better policy-making. As citizens and future leaders, we have to require, even demand for a *Better Leadership for Kenya.*

There is a better Kenya that awaits us, if we have the courage to choose different. It is a Kenya we can work towards, a Kenya that is almost within our grasp. It is time to pursue that Kenya. It is time to get rid of the cynicism that allows many of our citizens to suffer needlessly, while we fail to craft and implement policies that truly speak to the purposes of government.

It is time to elect leaders who *want* a better Kenya, who are *committed* to a better Kenya. This is a commitment to a better Kenya, a movement to change the lives and destinies of our fellow Kenyan citizens. It is an obligation we cannot shirk, that we have no choice but to fulfil. We owe it to ourselves, but more importantly, to those that came before us and made it possible for us to celebrate freedom, and to the future generations from which we have borrowed this beautiful country.

Chapter 2: Devolved Government

ଔଛଔଛଔଛ

1. What are the overall benefits realized by Kenyans as a result of Devolved Government?
2. Is devolution complete? Are there functions of the National Government that ought to be devolved?
3. What is the cost of our devolved government (especially absent new revenue streams)?
4. Is devolved government more beneficial than pre-devolution government and if yes, how?
5. Has devolved government been more efficient and effective at meeting and serving citizen needs?
6. Should Kenya reconsider the structure and outcomes of devolution with a view to revisions?

Introduction

The promulgation of a new constitution in 2010 represented the culmination of a long road in Kenya's quest to decentralize the power of a government that had grown too big, too distant and especially nonresponsive to the needs of citizens. It was a necessary course correction, not unlike those that occurred in and over time: independence, repeal of section 2 (a) and 2008's Government of National Unity (GNU)'s creation.

But in correcting government excesses, we inadvertently created new units of governments that are more akin to paper tigers, and that are rife with contradictions. This matter is discussed in proposals for potential future changes to administrative borders, but it is clear to most that devolution was far more complex than any – or most of us – had imagined. It has especially been challenging to citizens because of the cost but also the pandemic. Now, this latter could not have been foreseen, but it nonetheless was important.

Devolved government is expensive. Anyone who suggests that it is not is either doing the proverbial ostrich-head-in-the-sand, or their math is wrong. While it was not necessarily clear that the cost of the devolved levels of government were considered during the push to devolve Kenya's government, now we see the cost of devolution and the new institutions, structures and constitutional commissions it created.

Pitted against the overall benefits of devolved government and given that devolution did not come with a different revenue stream, the cost is clearer. Over a decade after it was first promulgated and two (and approaching three) elections later, it is clear that devolution is costly. What is not entirely clear is whether any cost-benefit analyses have shown that the average citizen has actually benefitted from devolution, or if the cost of more government is pushed onto their plate, requiring them to dig deeper tax-wise. One suspects that the latter is true.

There are many ways to contextualize and account for the success of the idea of devolved government. Yes, today there is a Senate, 47 Counties and their executives, 47 County Assemblies and 47 Women Reps. The latter is a most overdue correction – but the key question is whether *more government* is *better government*, or more *effective*. So even as we enumerate the outcomes of devolution by new offices created, it is not clear that the cost and standard of service delivery, the cost of living and other citizen-focused issues improved.

Here is a challenge to Kenyan citizens: consider any public policy, new rules, better rules or some improvement that can be directly attributed to the reality of devolved government. The skeptics among us regularly suggest that there are now more licenses to acquire, more taxes to pay to different governments with more conditions to fulfil – and no appreciable rise in income, quality of service, performance by civil and public services (except maybe more courts), or some other benefit that did not exist under the non-devolved governments.

It may thus be cynical to suggest we only devolved the number and distance to citizen, of fat-cats, corrupt officials, motorcades moving you off the already crowded roads (or in the sparsely populated areas, moving you off the road anyway even though there is fewer cars, bikes, motorbikes and maybe more cows and goats on the road), in a way that chase cars are a totally unnecessary expense?

Devolution may have thus created more visible, but not necessarily more efficient government that alleviated the burdens on Kenyans. It also did increase the number of taxes we have to pay and their cost. After all, wasn't the purpose of devolution to have better representation and better government? Perhaps the value of devolution and representation cannot be measured simply by the numbers or the cost. Or perhaps it can. How have Kenyan citizens benefitted by spending US$19.02 billion, or Kshs. 1.902 trillion over the past 10 years or so on 174 individuals? This is the cost of paying an additional 60 Members of Parliament (MPs), 67 Senators and 47 Governors whose offices were created by the

2010 Constitution. This does not include their offices' expenditure, or CECs.

Could this money have been used differently? If it was divided up between the almost 9,000 secondary schools (4,000 boarding) in Kenya, each school would have received a Kshs. 200.14 million lumpsum, or 21,133,300 per year. Dividing it by the total students enrolled in secondary school today, all 3.5 million, with an annual tuition of US$600 (or Kshs. 60,000 per year), each student would have benefitted from Kshs. 1,811 per year for the past ten years, and considering they only go to school for 4 years, it is likely to have been more. We essentially created a group of 174 individuals who take in substantive portions of government budget on salaries and allowances (excluding the CECs, staff and so on), and to what end? Better laws? Better government? hardly. This is not *A Better Kenya*.

Kenya is essentially an 'over-governed' country. 'Over-governing has especially had very significant impacts on the overall financial position of the country. And this has taken place in the middle of a new expansion of critical road, railway and port infrastructure and a pandemic. Infrastructure development, more critical but more useful than any devolved government could be, has increased the overall cost of government, without any commensurate new sources of revenue.

When the new governmental structures were put in place, it was not clear that the cost of such government was explained to most Kenyans or that they approved of the cost. Kenya was still a relatively less wealthy nation, and then we added on ourselves a 10-year, US$20 billion cost for no marked improvement in government and governance. Together with new projects, we've borrowed like there is no tomorrow. Maybe there is no tomorrow. We are borrowing against the future of our children and their children, to pay a small group of elites insane amounts of money, some of them to insult us.

And the pay (differential) is insane. Fr a long time, Kenya's legislators have been the second-best paid in the world. Kenya competes quite favorably with Nigeria. Considering that MPs make close to US$120,000 (or Kshs. 12 million) a year and the average per capita GDP for Kenya is US$1,400 or about Kshs. 140,000 a year, MPs are making almost 10 times what most Kenyans make yearly. In comparison, advanced and decidedly wealthier nations such as the US, which has a per capita GDP of US$60,000 – give or take – pays its legislators a mere three times the per capita GDP, at US$174,000. It would be one thing, defensible, even, if MPs were paid so much to make policies that improve Kenyans' lives.

To pay these persons and to also meet the infrastructure obligations, we have borrowed. *A lot.* It is useful to briefly mention Kenya's total debt and its rather exponential growth. In 2000, our total external debt stood at Kshs. 1.151 trillion. It rose to anywhere between 4.015 trillion to Kshs. 7.34 trillion in March 2021.[5] CEIC illustrates the kind of hole that we as Kenyans have collectively dug ourselves into. We have so far managed to amass a total government debt of US$ 71.5 billion.

Comparatively our Nominal GDP reached just US$ 24.5 billion in September 2020.[6] Other data shows that Kenya's total public debt increased by 16.8 percent during the one year period from March 2020 to March 2021.[7] Some of this debt is owed to China for programs and projects that started long before the COVID-19 pandemic, but we have that proclivity to borrow on top of existing debt. We are making some dent: Kenya's government expressed intention to restart payments, with an initial tranche of Kshs. 117.7 billion in 2021.

Another cursory examination of the debt servicing data is cause for concern. Of the previously mentioned Kshs 117 billion repayment, Kshs. 24.7 billion was interest alone. Indeed, although there are not many loan sharks out there willing to lend to us, we are essentially borrowing at almost 30 percent interest rate. Even this is modest: Herbling estimates that the cost of debt service surged by 35 per cent through June 2021.8

The country's overall debt service costs are projected to reach Kshs. 1.17 trillion by 2022, almost double the Kshs. 669 billion set aside for development projects.[9] Essentially, we learnt nothing from Zambia's 1990s situation at the height of the Washington Consensus' *terrible* advice. At the time, Zambia was estimated to have been spending approximately US$ 37 million on education and over US$1.3 billion in debt servicing and repayments, not creating the future human resources that would dig it out of an economic hole. Some data shows Kenya's debt to GDP ratio to have increased to almost 65.6 percent although according to CEIC data, the figure is even higher, standing at 68.8 percent as of September of 2020.[10]

There is an even more 'depressing' finding from cursory scrutiny of most data and applying some math to it. If one takes the approximate figure of US$ 1,400 per capita GDP as the true measure of Kenyans' aggregated annual income (which converts to about Kshs. 140,000) a year, and a debt of Kshs. 7.1 trillion for a population of 55 million, it becomes quite evident that we are saddling future Kenyans with unsustainable and enormously unfair obligations. Every Kenyan currently owes (internal and external debt combined and divided by the population), exactly Kshs. 133,962.26 based on currently available figures.

It is immoral to borrow so much money from the future to pay for the present, without taking some responsibility for why we are borrowing, and at minimum, committing to changing the present. What is also especially concerning is that we are borrowing money from all manner of places and suspicious lenders, so that we can pay salaries to the members of devolved government, and pay for their body-guards and security at their residences, to fuel patrol and chase cars, so that the elites can elbow us out of the way to rush to carry out...'important government business' even though more than almost half of them have been indicted for corruption, and none of their 'important government business' has especially improved the overall circumstances of Kenyans. We need a less indebted, financially better-managed Kenya, and before us lies very significant, if painful (at least for those with chase cars), adjustments.

The Recourse

By far the most efficient way of getting Kenyans to think about the cost of devolution is to consider the cost of government against the benefits that costly, expanded government brings. Since 2010's constitution, through public initiatives such as BBI and in debates, we have argued back and forth about devolved levels of government, whether the constitution should change to increase or decrease them, whether we should have more MPs or not, but we don't ask whether more government is necessarily and always better government. It is almost rhetorical to ask this: what were we trying to do with devolution?

We have flouted other provisions of the constitution. No one is advocating that this be the case, but the argument that pervades whether or not we should enforce the Two Thirds Gender Rule (or disband institutions that flout it) is excellent in one respect: if structures are not working, should we keep them just because they are in the constitution? Most argue that it is the quality of women's leadership, not the number, in the insistence that the Two Thirds Gender Rule is unenforceable. Perhaps more, or devolved government not being better, or even cheaper government ought to be subjected to the same.

One could easily respond that devolution aimed at bringing government services closer to the people. It is also worth asking what model of devolved government we adopted. Some suggest that it was a hybridized US-Kenyan-UK system. This may be the case but there are major and significant differences: in the US, there are states that might be equivalent to our counties, and in the UK, there are devolved governments such as in Wales, which make some decisions on their citizens but is still part of the UK, without a separate defense or foreign policy apparatus.

If that was what we as Kenyans had done with our version of devolution, or at any rate, intended to do, then we may have, inadvertently, made many and occasionally, grave omissions. These omissions make Kenya's devolved governments mere paper tigers. Our devolved governments, without bringing in any new sources of revenue, became another avenue, a financial black hole. They are efficient guzzlers of financial resources, but lack some of the most important powers held by devolved governments, powers that would make them more effective.

Structurally, Kenyan counties more closely resemble the idea of US states, which have an executive (governor and their cabinets), a state legislature (house and senate, often given different names, e.g., house of delegates) and control of a militia, i.e., the national guard. The latter might be equated with the county inspectorates, but with completely different functions. However, governors in and of states have a number of other powers that make states more or less fairly independent.

States can, as mentioned, raise militia. They can set state taxes, e.g., sales tax or state income tax (or decline to collect certain taxes, e.g., Florida). They issue state IDs, which are recognized by the federal government. They can regulate issues such as licensing of vehicles (produce number plates, also recognized by other states). They set inspection and emissions standards, issue fishing and hunting licenses, regulate building codes, run their education and accreditation departments and HEIs, especially higher education – institutions within their jurisdictions, regulate curricula and set state testing standards. They help to run federal grants and programs, such as Medicaid and TANF. They maintain certain state-level infrastructure, such as roads with the money they collect in taxes, but also get federal grants to run certain infrastructure such as Interstate highways.

The philosophy of the formation of states is also much different. US states *preceded* the federal government, so they had some modicum of the infrastructure that Kenyan counties aim to put in place, but as a following, not as a leading proposition. Most of their privileges, immunities and responsibilities are not found in Kenya. Counties have little to no recourse as to how to raise taxes, besides issuing business licenses, and this almost necessarily creates a race to the bottom: how does the county raise as much revenue as possible? While some develop businesses, some just gleefully restrict their roles to taxing their citizens.

One might consider that the VAT collected within the county might be remitted to the county, but some counties would then not afford chase cars. In reality, states have precious few sources of financing, other than business licensing. They are almost wholly dependent on the government, which finances their operations, including all the schools in their jurisdictions, hospitals, legislatures, (most) major roads and infrastructure and every substantive activity they engage in. It leads to questioning of the need for their existence. If counties had some leeway to raise revenues and to manage some of the *local* matters within their jurisdiction that do not have national security or foreign policy implications, that would give them financial flexibility.

This is not exceedingly challenging: such items as license plates affixed to county government vehicles already distinguish the counties. Why not extend that so that residents of counties can register their motor vehicles in the county and presumably, get that revenue to the county? Why not let counties raise money to run hospitals within their jurisdictions, or allow them to license industries? Or run other concerns that more directly relate to their residents? (This might be a terrible idea, just to be clear). If they did, it would soon become apparent which ones are effective and then, Kenyans would likely compete to live in a county that has the best 'quality of life.' To this extent, Kenya's devolution is essentially half-complete, and counties have little to no incentive to improve their governance. After all, why would it benefit them if they have an influx of citizens, which might only further impact their available resources?.

It is necessary, critical even, to rethink devolution. True, we have 47 counties, but it is necessary to ask whether the functions of devolved government needed counties, or if there was a different way to go about this. A country's - or more specifically, Kenya's - administrative regions should by design enhance the welfare of the citizens. It should, in theory, make it much more feasible to access government (local and national) services at the most minimal cost possible. If they are not, but continue to draw from the exchequer, they should be re-thought. Administrative units should not exist as a matter of expediency or to fulfill the National Government's whims over controlling citizenry; rather, they should only exist to the extent that they provide certain services to citizens.

One conspires to think that Huduma Centers actually provide most of the services that citizens require and that counties, therefore, are superfluous, and decidedly expensive. And Huduma Centers did not have to be built around the infrastructure and idea of counties. Indeed, just two centers per county would have been more effective than the devolution of government (and one might add, corruption).

Devolution has had some marginal benefits. Some new hospitals have been built, while older ones have been re-classified as Level 5, suggesting the highest level of care. Whether or not they have the facilities that denote their improved status is questionable. The queues outside of the hospitals suggest that this might not be the case. Courts have also been built, even though the backlog of cases has not especially decreased.

One famous lawyer made the valid point, that there is no way the president could have known everyone he appointed, despite that the structures were so set. The simile used was one of a bus driver. If the president (bus driver) was driving the bus, he couldn't always know what the pickpockets in the back of the bus were doing, hence devolution became a good thing, at minimum, by diluting the concentration of the power of the central government. It was sort of the least worst option.

Changing this reality of counties is not simple. It would essentially require a rewrite of the whole constitution, and given the level and number of invested persons in their existence, this sounds like a non-starter. However, just as Kenyans changed the constitution in 2010, the cost of the current structure of the nation is worth considering. It is not a decision that any one individual can propose, but the most powerful argument is likely the cost. Once citizens fully do a cost-benefit analysis of devolved government, one imagines that a different structure might emerge. On the other hand, counties can be strengthened, although such strengthening of the counties so that they can collect taxes in no way mitigates the cost issue.

The radius concept

Kenya is a vast country. It is unreasonable to expect that citizens can always access government services from the capital city, and woe unto them if the government official who they need to see is 'out to lunch.' That said, however, some services appear to only be provided there, particularly obtaining a passport. It has always been puzzling as to why we fail to fortify institutions and make them so robust – for example, the Huduma Centers that are to be found in each county – so that getting a passport is as easy as (in the US where one can) go to the post office, take a picture (they do), putt together your documents and mailing them, US$140 and your passport is mailed to you within six weeks? What's wrong with us, that we can't have systems that do such a simple task? It is almost unbelievable that government can continue to preside over systems that are innately weak, and not find ways to strengthen them for the benefit of wananchi.

Government has made access to its services much more easier online and one understands that there is, occasionally, a need to actually physically interact with the government. But Huduma Centers fulfill this duty quite well. It is necessary to examine just how much counties affect individuals. Is it more feasible to have double the number of Huduma Centers, and then allow citizens to get service from the Huduma Center that is closest to them by radius, and strengthen some Huduma Centers so that they provide even those more advanced and security-conscious services, such as passports? This is a path to a more efficient and effective service provision and seems a good way to access all government services more than counties do.

The Swiss Model

Direct democracy is rare, found nearly nowhere but ancient Greece and Switzerland. Switzerland is a more useful structure to contemplate, not just because it is newer and more contemporary. If you ask most Kenyans of the UK Prime Minister's name, or the US president, they will likely know. But do they know the name of the President of the Swiss Confederacy? It is highly likely one would need to Google it (By the way, his name is Guy Parmelin). There is a twisting path to the correct answer. But in this twisting answer, therein might lie Kenya's salvation. Kenya's, and that of many other nations that are linguistically and ethnically diverse and somewhat nationally disunited.

The Swiss Confederacy has 23 Cantons, with 46 representatives, 2 for each canton, who legislate in the Federal Assembly (Council of States). There is also a Lower House (National Council) with 200 members. The Swiss Presidency is Federal Assembly elects the Federal Council, a group of 7 'Councilors'. Each Councilor is tasked with running a department. It also elects what is essentially the 'chair,' the 'president' of the Federal Council, who serves as the president for 1 year. The president serves to represent Switzerland in international affairs and other executive functions. The Council also elects a vice president, who generally succeeds the 'president' of the Federal Council the following year. Confused yet?

If Kenyan leaders are honest and dedicated to the proposition of the well-being of citizens, and if Kenyans are determined to put paid to the very high-stakes game that is Kenya's politics today, the Swiss Model looks like a no-brainer, unless the goal of politics is to amass individual power, wealth and recognition. Granted, Kenya already has 47 counties (which one might consider cantons). Although the idea of a parliamentary democracy was rejected, and now that we have the counties, what if it was possible to take the counties, marry them with the 8 (former) provinces which would become the super-regions (or super-counties), or the 'departments' that correspond with the 'councilors' functions?

Then, ensuring a near-equal distribution of the number of counties per each super-region, Kenyans would be called upon to elect their governors in each county, and the county governors would elect one 'councilor' to the 'super-county' council? That way, we would end up with 8 super-county persons. To ensure that no one region is disadvantaged, we would move to either a 4-year term, or an 8-year term of office. The latter would allow each elected 'chair' (or president) of the 'super-county' to serve for one year. If a 4-year term was selected, 'super-county presidents' could serve for a period of 6 months' rotations each, with no one allowed to be elected twice during the same 4-year (or 8-year) period.

How would the 'councilors' be elected? This is the challenge, but one that is surmountable. In the Swiss Confederacy, the upper house, the Federal Assembly (our equivalent of the Senate) elects the Federal Council. For Kenya, it might be useful to have a two-step system. First, individuals would run for the regular positions (governor, MCAs, MP, Women Rep, Senator). Then, the 47 governors would have 8 of their lot elected (by a combination of the Parliament and Senate), for the 8 positions, with a geographical distribution (so for instance, governors at the Coast would vie to be elected to the super-county to represent the Coast), and so on, for each of the 8 super-counties.

Granted, there are a number of challenges to this approach. For starters, the issue of political domination by some groups might resurface, and the whole enterprise might become a schism along ethnic lines. There might be a consideration for this, although it is also likely that the electoral process would make this impossible. There are also good arguments for 'managed democracy' such as in Iraq, where the top positions are occupied by leaders from different ethnic and religious groups.

It is likely too, that quite a few people would be frustrated that they would not become president or president for more than a year, but the beauty of this is that within 8 years, 8 counties would have had a representative occupy the highest office in the land. Yet on the whole, this would offer each region a chance to gain leadership and allow for an evaluation of their efficacy during the rotating presidency.

Huduma Centers

If Devolution has not improved the lives of Kenyans – having Governors and MCAs who have not necessarily made laws to facilitate easier access to credit or farm implements, made trade easier, increase foreign market access through exports or other economic activities, made trade deals and agreements, it is useful to highlight one aspect of government that works better and is essentially what Kenya mostly needs to achieve service delivery efficiently close to the people: Huduma Centers.

A Better, Devolved Kenya

As constantly reiterated, this movement is not at odds with individuals; rather, it is the policy (or lack thereof) that it takes exception to. The President's final Address to the Nation suggested that BBI should be passed, and with it, new/other/top executive positions created. We disagree: Kenya does not need any more executive positions, each costing more than a total of 100 Kenyans' annual income.

What the country needs, and what would benefit us as a nation, is a change that makes it easier to represent the wishes, dreams and aspirations of Kenyans. While leadership is important, we as a nation can reject the hostage-taking that occurs every five years, where the political temperatures go up, and where citizens begin to wonder if we are headed down 2007/2008 again. We need to restructure the top leadership positions so that the stakes on the top position are less, and thus do not lead down the path to conflict. The country also needs servant leaders, who will consent to giving up their aspirations for the greater good of the citizens. This is something the country has lacked, and by that deficit, it is easy to see how little progress we have made to date. Individuals are important, but the collective is too. It is decidedly more important than any one individual's aspirations.

Devolved government may have its uses, including perhaps providing opportunities to distribute the benefits of political patronage, although this not necessarily in the best interests of the average Kenyan citizen. It is especially vital to consider the cost of devolved government, and to do a cost-benefit analysis. Kenyans already agree that the constitution might need a redo; there is no more urgent issue than reducing the cost of government, and restating the equality of all citizens.

To have our devolved government and thousands of leaders who earn lots of money and pay no taxes, get car grants and to have publicly-funded security, and then carve out constitutional exemptions for them, creating new offices just to keep them happy is the antithesis of a good leader. We should remember that Kenya was broke even before the 2010 constitution was promulgated. Creating new offices is just plain not the way to go. We need to consider the Swiss Model seriously.

Chapter 3: The Economy and Trade

ঙ৪৩ঙ৪৩ঙ৪৩

1. Why is our agriculture stagnant, dependent on rainfall and unable to even basically feed Kenya?
2. How can we build an economy for the future especially with the overwhelming youth populations growing up?
3. What is the role of education integrated with research and development to procure new economic opportunities?
4. Why doesn't Kenya diversify into other areas such as services, exports of human resource and utilize sports (athletics) as additional economic outputs?

Introduction: Economy and Trade

It is nearly impossible to speak of Kenya's economy without considering the role of agriculture, and the sheer number of Kenyans whose fortunes are tied to a sector as old as man's civilization. Even in this age of industrialization and information, Kenya's economy continues to be heavily reliant on agriculture, trade and tourism. FAO estimates that 26 percent of the GDP is directly contributed to by agriculture, another 27 percent of GDP is linked to agriculture. It is also estimated that 40 percent of Kenyans work in agriculture, of which over 70 percent of rural Kenyans work in the sector.[11]

This is almost 38 million people as of 2020, who were engaged in agriculture, considering 72 percent of Kenya's population lives in the rural areas.

Most of the agricultural production that is highlighted and that contributes to the economy is in subsistence farming. Estimates hold that up to 75 percent of all agricultural production is small-scale, subsistence farming and livestock production. Rather unfortunately, the practice of agribusiness has not taken off, and to-date, few large commercial firms and agricultural enterprises besides flower farms and poultry exist. Production is heavily reliant on previous-year seeds and rainfall, all of which have changed dramatically over the past 25 years, owing partly to climate change and a steadily, rapidly growing population. Unfortunately, previous Kenyan administrations have rarely outlined visions that promise to change these trajectories.

Taking the example of my own family makes clear that agricultural production on small farms is unsustainable in the long term. My father was allocated a 32 acre farm at independence – although he still had to pay certain amounts of money to the government throughout the first many years of our life on that farm. Since he had married 3 wives, he ended up with 13 children (which comes to about 4 for each wife, a small number by comparison to other families at the time).

In the immediate post-independence years, there were major attempts to improve individuals' lives, including by procuring loans for agricultural production. Over time, one became aware that he was paying off Agricultural Finance Corporation (AFC) loans, or money borrowed from the same, to undertake wheat farming, carrots, cabbage and potatoes, some of which were ravaged by environmental conditions such as El Niño and La Niña seasons. In the end, he had to sell off 17 acres of his land, to pay various debts and to educate his 13 children.

Ultimately, in his sunset years, he decided to divvy up the remaining land, which saw each of the wives acquire 5 acres each. Five acres divided up by 4 children came to about a little over one and a quarter acres. That was what I inherited. One of my brothers married 2 wives, and has 8 kids altogether.

If he were to divide up his 1.25 acres among his 8 kids, each will have a paltry 0.16 of an acre. It is most evident that there is no possibility of an individual being supported on such a small piece of land, especially if the children then have sizeable families. Further, when considering that 900,000 of the 1 million children (including my brothers') will drop out of school and not complete their educational journey, one is unsure how even an inheritance of land will allow for the continuation of agricultural production to even support oneself in future. This is a trap that Kenyan leaders must see and address before we reach it.

The present rate of dependence on agricultural production for both personal consumption and as an economic activity is unsustainable, and Kenya's primary trade goods such as coffee and tea have found major competition from nations such as Sri Lanka, Ethiopia and Colombia. It is necessary to make agriculture more efficient and productive, and less environmentally harmful and more sustainable.

Considering that now, 53% of Kenya's economy is directly or indirectly linked to agriculture, the Government needs to *urgently* design and implement programs that both support making agriculture efficient, through such initiatives as large-scale farming, agribusiness but more importantly, gradually shift away from the overwhelming dependence on agriculture. We propose a number of possibilities around this.

Diversification of Economy and Trade as GDP Sources
Employment

Today, unemployment across Kenya is estimated at about 40% of the population. This number has not changed since 2001, although it is exceedingly challenging to get an accurate tally of just how many Kenyans are unemployed. There is also a twin issue of underemployment, where an individual's spectrum of ability is not fully utilized especially in employment. For those who work in agriculture, if they do not actually pay themselves, even the 40% unemployment rate is an understatement.

It is necessary and urgent to employ especially younger folks, who make up almost 70% of Kenya's population or 20 million (for those aged between 14–35 years). This is far too many citizens. While in and over time we *have no choice* but to move our citizens from overwhelming reliance on agriculture as the primary economic activity, deficit spending to ensure food security by seeing to it that we empower youth in employment and investment in agribusiness will ensure Kenya meets its Strategic Food Reserves goal, but also give them income and forward—looking employment, hopefully away from the farm.

Kenya 'enjoys' a glut of labor and human resources, although it needs to restructure how these human resources are educated, so as to improve our global labor competitiveness. Simultaneously, we need to consider countries with high labor shortages, ageing populations and large diasporas, such as Italy, as a potential importer of Kenyan labor. Granted, this may run the risk of being an avenue for brain-drain, but there are other, less training-intensive professions that can be targeted.

Looking to other markets also ensures that Kenyan foreign workers are moving away from the Middle Eastern labor market which has been portrayed negatively in the press, especially over the past two decades. More Kenyans can then support their families and communities including through investments in business and property. Ultimately, this also reduces the unemployment rate, estimated at near–40 percent for most of the late 20th and early 21st centuries.

Employment improves the dignity of work, and the contributions of, by citizens to their own and their countrymen's welfare. If and when elected, and when such plans are in force, more of the 'human resources and economic re-energization plans will be articulated in greater detail, and as one of the priority areas of the future administration.

Employment in the services
Economic estimates from most global data show that services account for about 48% of Kenya's GDP. It is possible and feasible to increase the volume, amount and contribution of services to GDP. As an English-speaking country, Kenya is in an excellent position to take advantage of offshoring and outsourcing opportunities, especially of consumer services, such as medical transcription, customer service, call centers and other related, non–agrarian services for which Kenya is well suited.

This would allow for an increase in formal employment. It does however require better infrastructure, such as telephone and internet connections, ease in business registration and the removal of non–tariff barriers, ease of doing business and such facilities as stable electrical supply. The benefit of such expansion into the services would also mean the upgrading of infrastructure in the country, all of these being net positive outcomes for the country and citizens.

Remittances and Foreign Earned Income

Remittances are a critical source of foreign exchange and many families' livelihoods. Late in 2021, the Central Bank of Kenya (CBK) estimated that Kenyans sent home a sum of US$278.4[12] million, equivalent to Kshs. 30.6 billion. This is important foreign exchange coming into the country. It has continued to rise even with the pandemic, but has potential to increase further. Besides exporting human resources to other countries mentioned before, it is useful to find new avenues for getting more Kenyans working, wherever they might do that.

We shall aim to negotiate with foreign nations in order to include Kenya in temporary workers' programs, such as the H-2 temporary skilled worker program in the US. Whereas the relationship between Kenya and the US cannot be assumed to be and remain in good shape – for their elections have consequences, some not so positive for Kenya – our historical relations with them provide an avenue for such cooperation. Increasing the number of countries with which we have labor agreements can only be a positive for Kenya.

Tourism

If Kenya's wildebeest migration was once described as one of the 'new seven wonders' of the world, the country has done quite a terrible job of marketing the distinction or sustaining the wildlife. It is not enough to have great wildlife and a few safaris: it is important to tout these wildlife resources as if they were the equatorial pyramids. Kenya's tourism services should be at each trade exhibition, each international trade fair, and should be creating programs and apps that further help the world to interact with its proffering. Both the animals and landscape are to be celebrated, but notably (at least before COVID-19) the beach and the weather are a key attraction.

Kenya does an extremely poor job of marketing its territory and especially the tourist attractions: most Americans, who make one of the more resourced sources of tourism, tend to have precious little about Kenya, or the tourist attractions it has. True, it is a full 16 hours away from North America, but the experiences are magical and memorable. As a country, we should also make it our priority to stop mucking up the tourism market. 1997 and 2007 did us little favors. No one wants to go to a country with insecurity, conflict and raging civil war. Kenya's political situation needs to be stable and supportive of foreign visitors unafraid to be in the middle of war.

Devolved governments have wrought both opportunity as well as acres of confusion about Kenya's overall strategy in key sectors of the economy and especially tourism. We get that the different counties have localized interests, and have begun developing tourism markets. In the tourism scheme of things, the county is an almost miniscule element. No tourist leaves Italy, the UK, US, China or other countries intending to only visit Nakuru County or Kiambu County.

Whatever localized interests there are, tourism is a regional, even national issue. Without a coherent strategy, there will be but a patchwork of strategies and areas where tourists can go and revenue fights. It is necessary to remember that 'tour circuits' are a much better strategic organization approach than for each county to develop its tourist industry.

Circuits, such as the Central Sector stretching from Nairobi's National Park, together with other proximate facilities as the Aberdare Ranges, Lake Nakuru, Lake Elementaita, Longonot, Hell's Gate and other areas of interest ought to be considered as one such circuit. The coastal region, together with wildlife preserves such as Tsavo, Kilimanjaro, Lamu, the

National Marine Park in Malindi, the South Coast and other attractions form another tourism circuit.

In western Kenya, different attractions, lakes, wildlife reserves and other points of interest form a different circuit, while the north enjoys the same. Attracting tourists into the country is the responsibility of the National Government, but working with County Governments, there is great potential to increase the number of tourists coming into the country but also increase rates, reach and profitability of Kenya's domestic tourism..

Foreign Direct and Diaspora Investments

Foreign Direct Investment (FDI) is a critical part, and indeed source of any countries' foreign exchange. Many Kenyans in the Diaspora have a goal of increasing their personal portfolios, and remain closely tied to Kenya. However, the overall investment climate, compared to countries in which they reside in the diaspora, is more marginal. They might wonder why stuff doesn't work, and why they would invest in such places. The issue of corruption and (mis)rule of law dampens the readiness to invest. To this end, it is necessary to ensure that the rule of law is respected and followed, and corruption rooted out.

Many including this campaign's candidate frets over potential investments in real estate, since one is then likely to find that the piece of property they own also belongs to sixty (60) different people or is as much findable as the wooly mammoth. This state of affairs is untenable and cannot be the future of investments in Kenya. Whereas the issue of graft is dealt with in other sections, nothing is more important and necessary to increasing especially FDI and Diaspora Kenyans' investments than the confidence in the rule of law and reducing corruption.

It is our intention to return the country to the rule of law, to transparency in the conduct of business, to assuring that government systems that manage land ownership cannot somehow be corrupted, and to restore confidence in markets, FDI and diaspora investments. We recognize that this is easier said than done, but also, that corruption needs to be eradicated. Our movement and future administration does not believe that prayer is the cure for corruption; more needs to be done.

It is also necessary to do more to develop Kenya as a most attractive investment destination. Possible new strategies including for example, improving the state of physical infrastructure that allows for investments to thrive. Whether one a plot to build a retirement home or a block of flats, integrated infrastructure such as water, sewage disposal, roads and electrical supply are vital. These are pathways to a better investment climate in Kenya. Besides, all the knowledge that all the well-educated Kenyan business cadre holds will be useful in structuring a new, different, honest, more pleasant-to-invest and *better* Kenya.

Sports and Cultural Tourism

Kenya's cultural environment is replete with opportunities. On the one hand, cultural diversity often appears to be a source of schisms between different groups in Kenya. But what if it wasn't? What if a different world, a *culturally better Kenya*, is possible? Cultural diversity is one of the richest and best opportunities to leverage its diversity in a positive direction. Many societies and countries have cultural festivals, ranging from the mundane – the running of the bulls – to the most interesting ones such as the State of Louisiana's (or famously, New Orleans') *Mardi Gras.*

Many of these attract thousands, sometimes hundreds of thousands of individuals who also spend up to thousands of dollars on different elements of such festivals. Kenya can do the same. If each community had half a day of song, dance, stories, riddles, warrior games and other displays, a full three weeks of cultural festival would, could become a major attraction, far more than anything that the famed *Bomas of Kenya* is able to muster. Besides sharing culture with peoples of the world, it would help preserve for posterity, the rich diversity of all of the Kenyan peoples and their cultures.

Kenya is renowned for its sports prowess. It is the winningest country especially in terms of marathons and long-distance races. Kenya not only has the athletes with the talent to win marathons and other races, it also has the training grounds for it. These are coveted resources, which can be exploited for sports tourism. The long-distance track areas can be licensed as training grounds. Special entry permits for athletes, coaches and others who deign to use our high-altitude resources should be provided, at cost, to foreign nationals who desire to train in Kenya.

A better organized use of global sporting events during which most Kenyans are supported should be part of the sports culture and the tourism thereof. In terms of athletics, a future administration deigns to examine sports recruitment for Kenyan students into markets such as the US through the NCAA member schools, as well as the other college sports conferences.

It is true that the most benefit might be an education in the region of Kshs. 5 million per student-athlete, but the training and other outcomes that such programs bring are far more valuable in developing an increasingly well-educated Kenyan citizenry, besides the value they hold for Track II (or person-to-person and cultural diplomacy).

55

citizenry, besides the value they hold for Track II (or person-to-person and cultural diplomacy).

Chapter 4: Agriculture: Economy, Food Security & Innovation

CROSCROSCOS

1. As an agricultural nation, how can we assure food security for the country, especially ASAL and marginal counties?
2. How can we utilize innovation to improve and surpass the current food production, branch out into other industries and create a Strategic Food Reserve?
3. What are alternative economic activities that lend themselves to feasible transformation of Kenya's economy?
4. How can we leverage and expand agricultural services to diversify to other areas of production, so that current students do not have just agriculture to look forward to?

Introduction

Since the Paleolithic age – or creation, or the Big Bang – agriculture has been one of mankind's mainstays, perhaps mostly because it provides the sustenance he needs to survive. One of the most important elements of humanity is constant progress. It is progress that moved us from hunting, gathering berries and fruits to farming, domesticating animals for milk, meat and hides and onto higher levels of industry. While industrial production has been known to us for all two hundred years, some societies have made more progress than Kenya.

Of a population of about 330 million or so, about 3 percent (3 million) Americans listed their occupation as agriculture. There are many reasons to suggest comparing Kenya and the US is probably more of arrow-roots and caviar situation, but there is no law against learning from what works and doing things more easily. The next generation need not to spend years doing the same, back-breaking work my mother has done for over 60 years, to scratch out a meager existence. Better leadership moves Kenyans to other forms of industrial and economic production and a better Kenya.

There is, and should be, no bigger priority to the existential purposes of any leader, or any movement, than the eradication of the near-perennial hunger, and mitigation of drought. We blame the west for many things, often rightly so, but if we cannot do better than they did, if we cannot do the simple things, like eradicating hunger, what good is freedom? *Starving independence* cannot, should not be (in) our future.

We aim to build massive reservoirs, and to grow, under irrigation, a Strategic Food Reserve (SFR) which will only be swapped with more reserves on a regular basis. Within three years, we aim to achieve food security and in five, for the SFR to have at least 90kg of food reserve for half the country. This is our pledge towards a Better, Well-Fed Kenya, combating once and for all the depressing images of our fellow citizens starving, and their animals reduced to mere skeletons.

Sixty years after gaining independence, there is no defensible reason why Kenya continuously goes through hunger cycles, necessitating all manner of begging. Most recently, Kenya got almost US$9 billion in food aid from China. We can, and ought to depend on individuals to feed themselves but even those developed nations that find themselves in crises (for instance, the US during COVID-19) made available more assistance including through food-banks, but also through income support. But it is not an every-day, every-year thing. Granted, almost half of Kenya's 47 counties have ASAL-types of climatic conditions, but technology – agribusiness, irrigation, green-houses – allow us to overcome the issue of perennial drought and therewith, hunger. It is *necessary* to eradicate hunger. Indeed, it is almost criminal that we have not done so yet. Perhaps our over-reliance on rain and bad public policy and planning can explain our poor outcomes, but food security is, and must be, a matter of national concern and security. This is the path to *A Better Kenya.*

An administration that is committed to improving agriculture, to diversifying into agribusiness, to increasing agricultural exports, eradicating drought and to ensuring that a Strategic Food Reserve (SFR) is vital to Kenya's future and fellow citizens. Whatever policies have been in place by administrations past and present, they have not achieved these goals. We articulate a vision and plans to change the outcomes of the nation in the area of food security and availability, and economic improvements while also taking into account future environmental change challenges and opportunities.

Sustaining and Sustainable Agriculture: Irrigation, water harvesting and reclamation
Kenya experiences recurring cycles of floods and droughts. The floods especially procure mounds of rainfall, most of which simply goes to disuse. We should be harvesting lots of rain and preserving it in reservoirs, making greater utility of groundwater and if need be, add facilities to ensure pipelines transporting oil might be used to provide resources to enable farming, pastoral and other agricultural activities.

By relying on 'purposeful, directed agriculture,' employing use of technology to increase total food and animal production as some of the small-size, intense agricultural practices in parts of Central Kenya have shown, we will make far greater use of land mostly lying fallow, and decrease our now-dependence on rain. Together with the use of technologies such as mini solar power grids to power agricultural activities, we will approach the goal of sustainable agriculture especially in ASAL areas.

Besides the use of new crops and technologies, and increasing engagement with agribusiness, and reclamation of arid and semi-arid regions to make them more amenable to farming and livestock keeping, we shall develop expertise and hire agricultural extension officers. Given the level and extent to which Kenya's economy's is dependent on agriculture, it is necessary to provide expertise to farmers, and support them so that their labor is more productive, not just hard.

Working with county governments, we shall ensure that there are at least 1,000 agricultural extension officers, working with agricultural technologists, to improve the levels of production. Funding for agricultural support services will increase by tens of millions of shillings, and marketing of agricultural products vastly improved. Already, County Governments are building markets and improving on existing ones, but we will make agriculture more efficient and rewarding, so that our farmers' greatest outcome is not just feeding themselves.

Agricultural Diversification
As noted in the next section, Kenya's population growth has not been keeping up with food supply: the former is growing much faster. Land available for cultivation and pastoralism continues to decrease in size and productivity. Due to increases

in population, land is endlessly cultivated and not even allowed to lay fallow, as experts would most enthusiastically propose.

Reduced soil fertility requires even greater additions of fertilizer, crop sprays and other scientifically dubious strategies with unknown consequences in a fragile health system. Even then, the level of productivity has not increased significantly. Besides new crops and animal breeds, it is necessary to diversify crops planted. For this, we turn unfortunately to one of the probably only positive outcomes of Columbus' travels to the New World, the Columbian Exchange.

The Columbian Exchange brought new crops to the Old World, while introducing some of the 'old world' crops to the New World. Since some of these could grow with less amounts of rainfall and in marginal areas, the amount of land under farming increased greatly. Previously fallow land now came under farming of such crops as potatoes, sweet potatoes, and even new farm animals. Other countries have encouraged their citizens to undertake similar processes and programs.

This led to both diversifying diets and income. The range of crops grown in Kenya today is small, particularly those that contribute to long-term storage food-crops. We should borrow from the example of the Chinese, who after interacting with those returning from the New World, increased their agricultural output, increased acreage under cultivation and even saw a population explosion. Even Japan's Shogun at one point encouraged the Japanese to consume more meat, not just rice.

We shall invest in expanding the range of crops that are grown in various parts of the country, including in ASAL areas. Expanding the range of foods grown, harvested, dried, stored and reused as seed further ensures food security and income, while decreasing dependency on rainfall. New, high yield crops and new short-term crops will be especially encouraged and provided for as part of SFR and agribusiness investments.

Pastoralism: Efficient Directions?
Pastoralism in Kenya is both a socio-cultural and economic activity. Millions of Kenyans depend on this important sector, for production of meat, milk, hides and skins, wool and other side-products. Yet our pastoral systems, much like our agriculture, have remained tied to our past, and to less-than-optimal production systems. Improving agriculture includes pastoralism, both in the manner of production and long-term sustainability. Kenya has many opportunities to increase her exports abroad, even as in the west, non-GMO beef and animal products continue to attract more attention and bigger markets.

The methods of production in the ASAL areas are very inefficient. Providentially, they could multiply at least twofold with the range of targeted measures regarding efficient production, water harvesting, rainfall prediction, and use of purpose-grown-and-harvested-hay, and other economical but efficient methods. We need to shun the approach that suggests we can continue roaming the grasslands as our ancestors did when the population was probably only a quarter of what it is now, and the weather patterns had not been seriously impacted by man's activities around industrial production.

Whereas conditions in the highlands, western Kenya and other regions with predictable rainfall patterns are much different from ASAL areas, various other issues militate against good and efficient livestock-based economic production. ASAL areas have a myriad of activities, practices and beliefs that complicate citizens' lives and the economic production of livestock even more. Mobility among pastoral families in the north, north-eastern and southeastern plains and the tendency towards raising symbolically large herds is also impactful. These herds are often unsustainable and put pressure on pasture and water.

The cultural, rather than the economic value of livestock are additional challenging factors. It is especially important to interface with community leaders in order to ensure that as the world changes, our communities change with them, raise fewer but more sustainable and healthy animals. Sociocultural change is never easy, and this will not be either. But improving pastoralism including through new approaches that do not depend on the pastoralists moving from place to place in search of grazing lands and water is necessary, desirable long-term more productive for the citizens and the country.

GMOs, DDT and Carcinogens

Genetically Modified Organisms (GMOs) have obtruded upon the world in many forms. Where they have been used in crops and the like, they have increased food yields, produced hardy crops, and even improved food security. Kenya has seen the progressive encroachment by these crops and the related products, and one believes in the future, they will only increase, rather than decrease in use.

Simultaneously, some have alleged all manner of negative relationships between GMOs and health outcomes, including mentions of cancer. This is a more scientific debate, but it is necessary to be careful about the balance between GMOs and the possible hardier crops and food security they may provide and better health outcomes we can expect from organic foods. After all, even in the developed countries which use GMO products have significant populations who religiously pursue organic food regimens. That said, there is not a sound argument between starving and not using GMO foods. Beggars cannot be choosers and as long as we are begging, we will undoubtedly get food aid that is predicated upon GMO foods.

A downside of the use of certain agricultural implements, chemicals and other agricultural additionals such as fertilizers, weed killers and other sprays on the citizenry is a clear and obvious danger. Settlements resulting from the use of such products as DDT and other chemicals especially in the west, where these sprays were thought to be carcinogenic should cause us to shun the widespread use thereof. The cases of individuals paid to argue that GMOs are a potentially safe path towards food security also give us pause, but we should not dismiss GMO's promise.

We can, and will increase production without putting Kenyans at risk. Although makers of some farm chemicals have been sued for billions of dollars, it is unlikely that Kenya might benefit from these, and the potential medical cost of treating various cancers far exceeds any capacity Kenya might have now, or in the future, to do so. Instead of going the GMO / DDT / weed killers and other farm chemicals way, we should focus on sustainable, natural agricultural production that leads to better economic outcomes and food security, using the best, time-tested methods e.g., crop rotation and natural fertilizers.

Agriculture and the Economy

Kenya's agriculture is not far removed from Maslow's hierarch's first step: physiological needs. We are, and for a very long time, have been only just feeding ourselves, with the occasional assistance of other countries and through food aid. Sixty years after independence, and no matter how badly off the British left us, it has long been time to stop holding out bowls, begging for food. We will establish a Strategic Food Reserve (SFR) that is regularly replenished and can feed all Kenyans for at least 3 months.

We shall establish this Strategic Food Reserve through better, improved and efficient agricultural production, and through large-scale and agribusiness approaches, with significant investment in expertise and support for farmers. It shall also be the policy of the government to reclaim and introduce crop farming in marginal ASAL areas, so that both crop farming and the availability of water become a boon to assist in restructuring pastoralism, so that it supports the needs of pastoral Kenyans, and helps to expand our agricultural export markets.

This future administration will also gradually diversify from agriculture into other areas of industry. Current debates on economic models focus a lot on whether future Kenyan adults will ditch the tablet for a wheelbarrow, by giving youth and young people opportunities to build small businesses. These are interesting debates; however, our approach is one predicated on ensuring that we are creating an economy for the 21st and 22nd centuries, so that children need not follow in the farming footsteps of their parents, unless it's agribusiness and economically productive, where they are exporting food to the Arabian Peninsula and other regions, rather than Kenya leasing the land for agricultural use by foreign nations. There is no worse fate than for a child to only look forward to the same fate as their parent, but with less of everything: rain, amount of land, markets, money and even zeal for the economic activity.

Chapter 5: Women, Gender and Equity

ॐ஫ॐ஫ॐ஫

1. What is the place of women (and girls) in the dispensation that is Kenya today? Are all Kenyans, regardless of gender, treated equally, and have the same opportunities?
2. Have our attempts at gender equity worked, and what more (or less) needs to be done to assure gender equity?
3. How do our constituent societies support (or don't) the pursuit of gender equality between men and women?
4. Have we, since 2010, progressively implemented those constitutional provisions that improve the lives and conditions of women across the country?
5. As a nation constituted by micro-nations, what minimum changes (if any) do we need to make in order to achieve gender equity? How can we better achieve gender equity?

Introduction

It is impossibly controversial to purport to quote a communist, but when one is right, they are, even when they are a communist. The accurate observation that "Women hold up half the sky," is generally attributed to Mao Zedong, that erstwhile founder of communist – if now modern – China. He was red-right. Women hold up half the planet, perhaps more.

Since man would be extinct without them, it seems that more than half the sky is the more accurate answer. Women are the quintessential creators, nurturers, channels and harbingers of human conception, bearing children, essentially propagating humankind, but that is not all they are. In fact, while that might be the most important responsibility, women multitask very effectively, and often, arguably, better than men can.

True, men 'participate,' in the process, but for all our human advancements, even those tempered by the ethics and propriety of potential procreation via test-tube babies, women *are* the only current path to assure the survival of humanity. In fact, there is no doubt that they hold the most important functions of humanity. Humanity would not exist without women and so, there cannot possibly be a more important function. My own perspective is that men may reign, but women rule.

Whether we threat women as the quintessential 'guardians of mankind's existence' is another matter altogether. Especially in Kenya, it is not clear that we do. Granted, we do attempt to level the playing field, but we have not quite succeeded. Whether it's in leadership, opportunity, business, property ownership, right over the control of one's body, consent, decision-making or a host of other social, political and economic issues, we – in Kenya, Africa and many parts of the world – do not give women the full measure of ability and opportunity.

And we are definitely the worse off for it. It is the view of many that most of what men can do, women can do much better, faster and probably cheaper. So, why do we insist on operating inefficiently as society? Sometimes it is a matter of socio-cultural beliefs, and while these are part of who we are as society, it is also important to appreciate that change is the only constant thing. But, what is the history of women in most African societies, especially as it relates to leadership and contributing to the wellbeing of society?

Powerful Women, Influential Women through History

It is not like we would be doing women any favors, if they were able to exploit the full spectrum of all of their abilities. There is a great and long tradition of women being not only impactful leaders, but also builders of empires and mothers of nations. Whether one looks to Egypt's succession of queens, the tribal folks often identified as Berbers or even further south, they will find a host of women leaders who are celebrated today, for rising to the pinnacle of their societies and in many cases, leading their people to greatness against essentially insurmountable odds.

They include Egypt's Sobekneferu (thought to be the first head of state, 1806 BCE), Hatshepsut, Neferneferuaten, the seven Cleopatras (especially Cleopatra VII Philator, who was a consort to Mark Anthony), the four Arsinoes and the four Berenices, their almost-compatriot, Makeda, the Queen of Sheba, the Algerian Berber queen Tin Hinan, and Mina (or Amina) the Queen of Zaria, one of the six multi-ethnic, multi-religious Hausa Kingdoms that thrived in the 15th to 17th century. There was also the famously, sat-on-the-back-of-a-slave Anna Nzinga of the Kongo kingdom, and further east, the Ndebele queen, Lozikeyi, the successor to her husband, Lobengula.

There are those women of lore, some more mythical than real, e.g., Wangu wa Makeri, said to have ruled (men) with an iron fist until. The colonial period also saw women leaders taking charge all across Africa. They include such figures as Nigeria's Mme. Alimotu Pelewura, an influential fish-trader who helped organize market women in Nigeria to advocate for women's rights during British colonialism.

Other notables include one Mary Muthoni Nyanjiru, famous for using the 'guturama' tactic during a 1922 protest involving Harry Thuku, which was later replicated in South Africa ('To Walk Naked') and in the 1990s Kenyan *Saba Saba* protests. Wars of independence saw many African women lead armies or fight European oppression. We fondly recall (or do we) the likes of the coastal leader, Mekatilili wa Menza, who famously crafted and administration that almost rivaled those of the more developed nations of Europe, to their great surprise. Others included (Field Marshal) Muthoni wa Kirima, Mukami Kimathi and Wambui wa Kanyari, centrally involved during the Mau protracted Mau rebellion leading to Kenya's independence.

Immediately after independence, luminaries such as Mabel Dove-Danquah and Grace Ogot were elected to parliaments or held other important positions in government. Soon, the women of power became presidents and Prime Ministers in nations all across Africa. They included Ellen Johnson Sirleaf (Liberia), Joyce Banda (Malawi), Ameenah Gurib-Fakim (Mauritius), Agathe Uwilingiyimana (PM and president of Rwanda for a few hours in 1994), Maria das Neves (São Tomé and Príncipe), Cissé Mariam Kaïdama Sidibé (Mali, PM) and Mame Madior Boye (Senegalese PM).

There were more: they included Saara Kuugongelwa (PM, Angola) and Netumbo Nandi-Ndaitwah (Deputy PM, Angola), Jewel Taylor (Liberia, VP) and Isatou Njie-Saidy (The Gambia's VP). In this regard, Kenya actually stands as one of the countries with the worst record of elevating women to positions of power – besides the Chief Justice. Even Somalia had a Deputy PM, Fowsiyo Yusuf Haji Adan, in 2012.

Others steered the ship of state in acting capacity. They included Slyvie Kiningi (Burundi, acting; also, one-time Prime Minister), Rose Francine Rogombe (Gabon, interim), Agnes Monique Ohsan Bellepeau (Mauritius, acting), Carmen Pereira (Guinea-Bissau, acting), Adiato Djaló Nandigna (acting PM, Guinea Bissau), Cécile Manorohanta (acting PM, Libya) and Catherine Samba (acting president, Central African Republic). Others succeeded presidents – albeit male ones – e.g., Tanzania's Samia Suluhu Hassan, or were elected on their own merit, e.g., Ethiopia's president, Sahle-Work Zewde, who was elected by the National Assembly. There are others who are almost equally illustrious, such as the tree-planting, social-justice warrior, Nobel Peace Prize winner and Kenya's own Wangari Maathai, and Sudan's 'Nubian Queen' Alaa Saleh, who rose to note during the 2019 Sudan protests.

Beyond the more regional and continental figures and closer to each individual is a class of most important women: mother, wife, daughter, and the other more expansive list that includes sisters, nieces, fiancés, girlfriends, *'mpango wa kando'*, ex's, friends, crushes, 'could have beens', *et cetera*. But this almost needlessly simplifies the life-giving, life-nurturing role of women in our lives: they are the custodians of life, of society, of our collective existence.

Women are not simply to be 'included' in development; they drive it. They are central to anything that a nation can hope to be. True, a nation's youth are its future, but more than that, its women assure the future, and some women are also youth. It always presents a most curious thought exercise, to imagine what might happen if *all* women around the planet decided not to have children for 30 years. *That* is really how important women are and should be treated.

Kenya's Troubled History – with Women

Kenya's history with women is troubled, to say the least. We do not treat women well, at all. Almost every metric tells us we are doing terribly, and we are doing so terribly that we needed to write into our constitution that we are going to assure the rights and place of women in the country. Even then, we still appeal to tradition in order to deny women the God-given equality owed them, despite our clear dependence on all they are.

But rather ironically, we then decided that women could (until 2010) inherit property from their fathers on occasion that they were likely to get married. A few years later, we decided that women had no right to enjoy the singular attentions and subsequent marriage by their existing spouse. We briefly considered whether or not their consent, even permission, was needed before their spouse was able to marry someone else. It occurred to some that if all Kenyans were indeed equal as the 2010 constitution suggests, the bill should have made polygamy *and* polyandry legal. The UN was one of the rather high profile entities to condemn this clear discrimination.

By the numbers, Kenya's performance is dismal, especially in equality and assuring equal treatment and protections under the law. To this end, one might suspect that there is a deeply troubling misalignment between the law of the land and the 'peripherals' that are often associated with socio-cultural traditions and beliefs. Nothing, for example, should be able to justify the marriage of an 11-year old girl to a man twice her age.

Socio-cultural traditions cannot justify human rights violations. We also cannot selectively abandon some of the most troubling elements of our socio-cultural traditions, such as those that especially discriminate against women. Many disagreements have come my way only due to the fact of pointing out that most developed, western societies, do not practice dowry, and no sort of malice comes to them. Every statistic shows a correlation between domestic violence and payment of dowry. In some societies, the phrase for paying dowry is "we are going to buy so-and-so." That should trouble us.

The other numbers, and reports, are truly calculated to induce shock, or as a nation, we have far to go. The frequent stories in the news, for instance the Murang'a man who collected almost 30 of his friends so that they can FGM his wife was shocking, but it was hardly the only highly troubling event. Most do not make to the news. But here, the science – yes, science – is clear. There are no benefits to FGM other than suppress women's right to bodily autonomy and keep up with tradition.

In this instance, the harms so far outweigh any possible benefits that everyone who contemplates it should be dumped in the ocean. Kenya's GBV rates are anywhere from 47 percent, which is an inordinately high level of violence. On the other hand, it almost makes sense that if we have 'bought' our women spouses, we 'own' them, and can do as we please. There is nothing probably more offensive in this land than GBV; that it still exists is an affront to us as a republic.

It is often not possible to legislate what ought to be. Arriving at gender equality ought to be a national conversation, in which we fundamentally assert that a) we truly hold all persons in Kenya to be equal, men and women; b) we will actualize the nation's objectives by applying this belief. We can legislate all we want, but until communities can see that it is in their interest to treat all their members equally, socio-cultural traditions will always stand in the way.

The 2010 constitution assures the equality of all men and women, but considering the poor representation at leadership levels and the obvious inequality, we find that inequality is just a mirage. This is true, especially if you consider the Gender Inequality Index, and the troubling denial of rights attributed to socio-cultural reasons. For example, the lack of frameworks or rights to inherit property or the dispossession of women is often supported by purported socio-cultural 'realities.' Polygamy is clearly discriminatory application and ought to be deemed to contradict the proposition of equality of men and women.

Whereas it would be a wonderful world where we could appeal to science to drive decisions, or at least subject them to rigorous and empirical investigation, that is unlikely to happen. It is not evident that one can oppose dowry or inequality on the basis of science. But a nation such as that which discriminates against its women has to understand that talent and intelligence are not gendered: discriminating women also harms *men,* and therefore, in the interest of self-preservation, it is not only fair, but necessary to capture the awesome abilities that women possess, beyond assuring survival of species.

Indeed, history bears this out: some of the best-known scientists were women (e.g., Maria Cunitz, Polish polyglot, or Sophie Brahe, far smarter than her brother astronomer, or Gabriele du Chatelet, far more productive than Voltaire, her intellectual companion). The discrimination against individuals, just because they are women, robs us some of the best sources of growth and development, and Kenya must endeavor to NOT be that nation. It is critical that we consider how we aspire to equality, not just in text, but in practical application.

Current realities

Today, both constitutionally and legislatively, Kenya has made some strides to assure greater inclusion of and participation by women more broadly in society. None is more notable than the two-thirds gender rule, even though its implementation has been wrought by disagreements over the practical challenges of implementation, or how to get at least one third of women, especially, to get elected to office. In particular, given the socio-cultural beliefs around leadership among significant portions of the country, where leadership is considered more of the domain of men, achieving gender equality even through constitutional and legislative provisions has not been easy.

We ought not to only be the prophets of darkness and despair. There are achievements we can be proud of, including the Women Enterprise Fund, under the Ministry of Public Service, Youth & Gender Affairs, the Uwezo Fund, which allows youth, women and persons living with disabilities to engage in entrepreneurship to foster economic development. Private organizations have also been at the forefront of working with women to improve their lives, including, for example, the Kenya Women Microfinance Bank (KWFT). Politically, there has been some marginal improvement in the levels of participation in politics. But none of these have necessarily generated gender equality. Over time, it has become evident that – even at international levels – mere programs and declarations cannot by themselves create equality. After all, wasn't it a president who spoke derisively of Beijing 1995?

As a nation, we must empower women today, urgently. We must also invest in girls and young women, removing those barriers in culture, which in free trade might be considered NTBs. Our socio-cultural traditions often function as NTBs, especially those that allow for arranged and early marriages, disinheriting women and denying them the opportunity to achieve their full contributions. Women get discriminated against even in such issues as naming rites and protocols.

We ought not to hide behind our pasts, or ascribe some of the unacceptable things that we do to culture, only so that we can continue to oppress women. A recent purchase of exercise books demonstrated the extent to which we are disenfranchising girls of the reality of what they can be: individuals depicted as lawyers, engineers and pilots were all men; nurses, teachers and traders were women. We must equip little girls with the confidence to be engineers, pilots, chemists, doctors and lawyers.

Future possibilities

Girls have come a long way in the area of **education** in Kenya, going from one-time not getting any education, to becoming one of the most educated groups in Kenya. There are pockets that still hold that women's education is a waste, despite all the HDI outcomes evident in women's education. Still, at the top levels of the education hierarchy – from the ministry to tertiary education – men dominate the profession, infrastructure and system. Girls can, and do see the examples they are set to emulate. It is challenging to ask one to be that which they have not seen. The elevation of – decidedly eminently qualified – women to positions of authority, including in engineering, law and justice (as was recently the case) is important, and goes some way towards meeting the two-thirds gender rule. Professors, guidance counselors and others who interact with girls in their formative years would go a long way to encouraging them to become everything that they can become.

Consensual, cross-gender **relationships**, the majority of relationships in the country, are another area in which gender (in) equality is troubling. That Kenyans are still debating and passing polygamy legislation in the 3rd millennium is scandalous. There are those issues in which we must evolve, or we will become dinosaurs. We have largely given up wife inheritance, FGM, leaving twins out in the forest on occasion that they are a bad omen, and many other ancient rituals that made little, if any sense, even though this June a story on the news about a woman who was dumped because she had given birth to twins indicated we have a ways to go.

We ought to now deliberate such issues as polygamy, naming rites, dowry and other issues that denigrate the life and value of women. Especially the issues of women's bodily autonomy, consent and right to choose (including a partner), freedom from GBV and severe penalties for perpetrating the same, prosecution of such issues as marital rape, and dedicating the nation to be advocates for gender equality are especially important paths to follow in future.

The issue of marriage, bride-price, marriage settlements and **dowry** are also at the crux of the consummation of marriage in many societies. Whereas there have been arguments of the role that dowry plays in making one a 'truly married woman,' fostering positive relations between families and groups (and now different communities) important, but just as we have found alternatives to FGM, it is important to consider whether these are the *only* or relevant ways in which such appreciation can be expressed. One suspects that it is not.

Dowry and bride-price had a place in the agrarian society of the pre-colonial era. It is unclear whether this vestige of pre-colonial life is necessary today, given that its original intent was especially economically motivated. Because especially dowry is an economic transaction and correlates directly with GBV, it is necessary to determine whether the idea of 'buying' someone contributes to such violence and thus, ought to be revisited.

Nothing is perhaps more important for the socio-economic well-being of women, which one surmises can be accomplished through **business** and **entrepreneurship** and access to **capital**. Because most financial institutions require collateral to obtain financing (e.g., title deeds, log books and even other tangible property), and since women are especially excluded from property ownership either by law or communal practice, the ability to start a business is especially constrained.

But, Grameen Bank showed us the importance of social capital as a foundation for economic independence among the 'unbanked' and those with little in way of property. Women were able to leverage collectivism in order to obtain funding. This is highly valuable especially when women have and run SMEs and small businesses. That there is a Women Enterprise Fund, which loans to women, is impressive; however, it is necessary to couple the funding with financial literacy training so that the businesses started with such funds can thrive and expand. It is also necessary to find solutions, through stakeholder involvement, to resolve discriminatory funding.

There already exist vehicles that can serve as a basis for business, entrepreneurship and access to capital, and an equally important function: **leadership**. Rotating Savings and Credit Co-ops, or ROSCAs, already exist in Kenya (and many other places). Most women belong to a "group" or a "chama." These have existed since time immemorial, and provide not only a collective approach to obtaining certain things from household items to starting businesses.

But over and above providing household cutlery, ROSCAs create 'social capital', which has been shown to allow groups more leverage in accessing formal channels for capital. They also provide leadership: the groups are often led by chairs, secretaries and treasurers. This is a ready pool of leaders who can be educated and nurtured, and expanded so that these leaders can be recruited to run for political office.

Aspects of **socio-cultural traditions** that negatively impact the welfare of women ought to be reviewed with an eye to resolving the contradictions between the constitution, which assures equality between men and women, and the practices that deny women the opportunity to exercise the full spectrum of their rights and privileges. Early child marriages, arranged marriages, FGM, dowry, denial of inheritance rights, domestic and gender based violence and perceptions of leadership have been an especially significant challenge and deserve a national conversation, especially since some communities are at risk of getting left behind, or challenging the rule of law and human rights as they assert communal and societal traditions.

There are other necessary and urgent concerns that can advance the position of women in the country, including, for example, public-private partnerships that allow legal training so that women can access more resources so as to obtain justice. Whereas private organizations do a good job of sensitizing their clientele, government ought to recognize the significant challenges that women face due to the combination of the factors above, and put in place strategies that mitigate those long entrenched beliefs and practices that diminish women's lives.

It has an obligation to emplace a strategic, focused department in the Attorney General's office to facilitate these issues, as well as encourage pro-bono legal services so as to level the playing field. It is also necessary for both national and devolved governments to ensure that they are unequivocally committed, in word, deed and policy, to gender equity and to support of women and the girl child.

Chapter 6: Critical Infrastructure

ॐॐॐ

1. Why does Kenya not have a coast-to-coast highway (not the one-lane-per-direction) motorway (A104) across its most populated areas even after 60 years of independence

2. What role has the lack of infrastructure played in the underdevelopment of the country for the past 6 decades?

3. What is the critical infrastructure (roads, rail, electric) that the country needs in the next 5-10 years to facilitate its approaching the LMIC we covet?

4. How ought we to understand public-policy and its decision (including not connecting landowners with electricity despite having titles to land) and what ought to be the new directions in this critical area?

Introduction

The past 10-15 years has seen Kenya go on a building spree; it has built acres of new infrastructure, encompassing roads, railway, airports, ports and connected most schools to the national power grid. This is a great improvement on the first 50 years of independence, when roads to nowhere were built, and airports where goats roamed the runways and grazed the well-kept grass and neighbors dried their maize on the same runways. It is not quite evident if the drying-maize is just a rumor but it's humors.

The roads that were built tended to fall apart before they were commissioned, and were mostly a little more than cattle tracks. When the first highways were built, they were highways to nowhere, although they did mitigate congestion in the approaches to the city center. These included Thika Road and the Nairobi-Limuru road. It was a good idea, but it was woefully insufficient, limited and essentially, akin to the 'road to nowhere', even with the reality of the capital region being the most economically vibrant in Kenya.

Kenya's infrastructure needed upgrading for most of its post-liberation existence. That the only railway line in the country before the construction of the SGR railway was built by the British (other than the private, short-run Lake Magadi railway), and whose trains were dubbed the 'Lunatic Express', is not to be celebrated. The construction of the SGR is important, but in real terms, this is akin to someone ditching walking, so that they can use a bicycle, when there are self-driving cars and even personal jetpacks. It is *inadequate*.

Countries such as China, Japan and France have high speed express trains, and while it is the case that we want to learn to crawl, then walk, before we run, there has never been any utility in reinventing the wheel. A high-speed train from Mombasa to Nairobi would take a little over one hour. One could literally live in Mombasa and work in Nairobi and vice versa. But our infrastructure is more than railways.

A Note on Telecommunications: Lessons Learnt
There is a famous saying that 'the dinosaurs became extinct because they did not adapt.' Nowhere does this saying apply more than in the fate of the Kenya Posts and

Telecommunications Corp. There was no amount of putting lipstick on a pig that could have saved KPTC/Telkom, and one would think that other parastatals (or state-owned enterprises, SEOs) such as KPLC/KenGen would know this, or would have learnt from the inertia that Telkom experienced prior to the explosion of new mobile telephony, and the really poor fate that befell it.

Telkom used fixed technology, telephone poles and lines. Getting a fixed line was seen as both prestigious but also more painful than pulling *all 36* teeth absent anesthesia. In the meantime, as early as 1983, the future of fixed telephony was in peril: the first mobile phone call was made. KPTC / Telkom didn't get the memo. And so, phones remained out of reach of most Kenyans, and government refused to liberalize the sector. They finally did, and every worst possible outcome came true. Telkom refused to go to school and learn new skills, and as such, once KenCell and Safaricom had their foot in the door, all the tears in Kenya could not save Telkom.

Like that proverbial ostrich, Telkom resisted technology and change, and made Kenyans beg for phone connections. As of 2019, the number of businesses and households with a fixed phone (landline) was estimated to be between 240,000 and 320,000. Rather belatedly, it began expanding the availability of phones, but it was more of the chicken/coop, horse/barn situation. When Safaricom launched the short-lived 'simu ya jamii', Telkom still refused to learn. Wireless technology really did kill it. Who would subsequently opt for a landline that you had to leave home when you could go to the *Shamba* with your phone? Now, Kenya's mobile penetration rate is over 110 percent.

The same fate can be seen to have befallen KBC, derisively dubbed the KANU Broadcasting Corporation. The proliferation of FM stations with hip ideas and audiences and music made KBC another has-been. The difficulty obtaining TVs and VCRs also gave Kenya one of its most interesting technology jumps: VCRs really never caught on, and when they might have, they were quickly over-taken and replaced by CDs and DVDs. Technology changes, whether we embrace it or not. Sadly, electrical power generation is likely to go the same way, because KenGen and KPLC cannot stop the proliferation of mini-grids, and if they do, they still can't beat solar power with solar batteries and mini power-generating stations that are essentially in a box. Kenya does not need to learn from all the bad outcomes especially if it can avoid them.

There is an inertia that has afflicted SEOs, one that stems from perhaps the enterprises being funded by government so that they essentially will be propped forever, even though they are essentially loss-making entities. One has to then consider how much loss they can take in exchange of 'prestige', prestige over having a national airline that barely flies or makes money or both (not Kenya), or being the sole supplier of petroleum and electrical products and services *and still making loss.*

Poor Infrastructure Management: Rail transport
Nothing is perhaps more ridiculously operated than the pre-SGR railway transport, especially in the capital, Nairobi, and its environs. No one can possibly forget the twice-a-day run of the train, and the commuters running full speed, helter-skelter, all over the city in the direction of 'Railways,' to catch the 5:15 train. Or the commuters who would risk falling off the train just to get on the train to and pay the Kshs. 20, or if they were *on top of the train*, the conductor likely got nothing.

Of course, it made sense that it was inexpensive to ride the train. What no one necessarily considered was that it would be *also* less dangerous and much better for everyone involved, riders, conductors, operators and the government, if most people were *inside* the train, and the train was not so crowded that the conductors could not possibly collect the fare inside the train. There was no thought of even asking them to collect the fares that were riding *on top* of the train.

It is likely that the train took all of 2.5 hours (from 6 a.m. to 8:30 a.m.) to get from Thika to Railways, but by that logic, it would have made sense to start a train at 5 a.m., another at 5:30 a.m., another at 6 a.m., another at 6:30 a.m. and another later, for all the citizens who did not need to report to an office at 8 a.m. In the evening, it would have equally made sense to start one at 4:30 p.m. through 7 p.m. But nobody asked me, so all the trains were jammed with commuters hanging on precariously, and some sitting on top of the train. The government lost money (no conductors could clamber onto the top of the train) and so, there is no way this even made sense.

Today, the SGR has replaced the 'Lunatic Express' towards Mombasa. In the other direction, towards Kisumu, new train service (or perhaps, new, old train service) is newly active between Nakuru and Kisumu, as of December 17th. That it has taken this long to revive the train service is scandalous, and further, that the 'new' railway runs on a 123-year old track is mildly concerning, but also, in reality, one of the first runs of the new trains in service came to a screeching halt only on its second run towards Kisumu. Smack in the middle of the most lucrative and busy holiday season.

There are plans, of course, to extend the SGR all the way to Kisumu, and this is noble. Once again, that Kenya took this long to think about new train service is shameful. For all their faults, and their clearly extractive-driven intentions for East Africa, the British *first* built a railway track. Perhaps the Kenyan government would have considered doing so, and ensured that economic development would proceed apace. Our public planning strategies are woefully inadequate, even in sectors as critical as transport, energy policy or even the more acute healthcare.

For the city especially of Nairobi, it is implausible that we still do not have regular commuter trains that can function well and for long periods. This is as confounding as is the sporadic service's loss-making, when it is a monopoly and full of commuters each train that is put out there. It is possible that we absolutely have no coaches, or engines, or train drivers, who can run train services along the existing lines, to Thika, to Kibera and along the Nairobi-Naivasha railway. It is also likely that the government did find out that it was not good in doing anything resembling running public transport systems.

After all, the well-known KBS (Kenya Bus Service) and NBS (Nyayo Bus Service) all came to an inglorious end. There is something to be said for contracting successful transport firms and managers. It is unclear if long-serving bus companies (everyone was familiar with Eldoret Express, Coast, etc.,) might have been able to contribute expertise to running the train service or not, but again, as Kenyans, when we view everything as a milk cow rather than a public service, we are destined to have the worst public transport – perhaps except Burundi.

Road Transport
One of the goals of this campaign is to foster a culture of public policy, deliberate and deliberative decision-making in the public interest, including by soliciting public input, opinion and contributions through public hearings, much as government should function. Again, few Kenyans have been asked, but there is a glaring, perhaps sectoral or institutional policy gap that

makes one wonder how policy is made, and who it is that comes up with such terrible public policy ideas.

Road transport is equally messy, although conditions have improved, and hopefully, with the new highways and express lanes, traffic and congestion will decrease. Some of the changes and new roads already make travel easier, but there are gaping bottle-necks. Also: we should probably desist from calling one-way almost-roads 'highways.' They are not.

One road would have changed Kenya's fortunes, had it been constructed. If it had been constructed in 1964 as a dual-carriage highway, a road from Mombasa to Kisumu would not only have changed Kenya's transportation infrastructure, urbanization, trade and overall development, it would also have brought in a lot of foreign exchange funds because Uganda, Rwanda, Burundi and eastern then-Zaire would have used it in transportation of their imports by sea.

Further, such a railway line and service would have locked the advantages of transportation through Kenya, thus favorably competing against then-Chinese-funded Tanzania. There is no fathomable reason, other than sheer lack of public policy planning and perhaps vision, that we do not have an east-west (or more precisely, a highway from Mombasa to Kisumu and Busia), and also possibly a south-north highway. Even before constructing the SGR, it would have made more sense to build a highway from Kisumu to Mombasa and from Namanga through Nairobi to Moyale.

What the public works, roads and such ministries did, why they continue to draw pay from the public exchequer when they do not even publicize and promote such infrastructure projects with life-changing implications is beyond comprehension. They did not build roads, or railways, or many public works. They did not even ensure that the few roads were not being destroyed by overloaded tractor-trailers. Ministries and bureaucracies should not just exist to exist, but they have to be especially functional, and justify their existence.

They can, and do have a portfolio that includes the policy-making elements of physical infrastructure, if not the construction elements (government might be just as terrible at construction as it was running buses). However, it is necessary to enforce the law, especially on axle loads. There is no point in spending millions – in some instances, billions – to build roads only for them to buckle within a month or less than a year. It reminds one of the days of Kirinyaga Construction and the state of roads in the 1990s and early 2000s.

Our roads are now better, but even their construction continues to be a puzzle. No one places bumps 9or speed limiters) on expressways or highways. There are footbridges, yes, and we should educate the Kenyan public of the life-saving utility of such bridges so that bumps become unnecessary. But, a second issue was not addressed.

In the major industrialized countries, in cities with lots of traffic, and this would absolutely work for Nairobi, most major highways have 'express lanes.' These are alternatively known as 'HOV' lanes (HOV for High Occupancy Vehicle). Imagine how much time would be saved, if a matatu filled with passengers in Thika (or Athi River or Limuru) and drove straight, on a no-bumps, no-stop express lane? These lanes would be reserved for buses, matatus and vehicles with more than 2 persons. It would make traffic flow even better.

It is also essential to consider the state of the major roads in the country, which ought to remain in the jurisdiction of the national government, if only for their national security, military and other related applications. If and when we get to a place of building actual highways – rather than the two lane blacktops we call highways – we can use them to honor Kenyan heroes, both men and women. There is nothing especially enlightening about having a highway named A104 or C67, especially when we could name them after those Kenyans who have made such significant contributions to Kenya

There are many arguments for renaming the highways, and this can be one of the areas in which the County Assemblies have some input, particularly with the transportation networks that are within their jurisdiction. This goes too, for most of the other infrastructure that bears the names of non-African personalities. There is no reason why Lake Victoria still bears that name, given the torturous history Kenya has with the former colonial power. After all, we renamed everything else, why not the remaining A104s and Lake Victorias? Indeed, this is one of the Britishy things that we still inexplicably retain.

Water: Harbors and Transport

Most of Kenya's population is generally unaffected by water transport. Those areas that are, have relatively poor transport infrastructure, especially at the coast. Water transport services have been long ignored, with repeated attempts at only utilizing ferries, ships and boats even when these are the less optimal transport option. The rest of the world has moved on to draw-bridges, high-rise bridges and bridge tunnels. We have not, but this (old technology) is perhaps somewhere in our future.

We are often reminded of ferry transport and its woes, especially at the Likoni Ferry, during major incidents, for instance the loss of MV *Mtongwe*, or during the COVID-19 pandemic's early days of curfews when Kenyans had to both social-distance and be home by 7 p.m., in what became one of the darker chapters of the pandemic.

Today, an estimated five ferries, MV *Harambee*, MV *Nyayo*, MV *Mvita*, MV *Pwani* and MV *Kilindini* are in operation. However, the overall safety of the ferries is questionable. The fact that the US has an advisory against using the ferry services really does illustrate the questionable safety. The proposed Dongo Kundu bypass is a good idea, and once completed, will especially be helpful in decluttering traffic in a most critical region.

But we should also aim to construct a tunnel and bridge (bridge/tunnel), part underwater, and part over-water, so that ships can pass through and cars can pass through the tunnel, or at any rate, a high-rise draw-bridge, which would allow ships to pass through, but which is more disruptive. These types of infrastructure projects have already been shown to work, including some of the longest ones in China and the US. China already built some samples with the SGR train.

Overall, the issue of water-related transport, as a national issue, is perhaps less critical, but it is important to those who use these means of travel. We have to invest in the building of bridges and tunnels, but also, in improving the overall safety standards of water transport, even on lakes such as Victoria and at the coast. Inland, we have to consider our relationship with water and the many water bodies.

Every year, during the long, and occasionally, short rains, transport is interrupted, people, bridges and animals washed away. It is important to take an inventory of all of Kenya's roads, bridges and any tunnels, in order to ensure that these are not washed away and people marooned. It is especially important to find ways to track run-offs in order to conserve water and to use it for other purposes, such as irrigation.

Electrical Grid

One of the most frustrating experiences of Kenyans is with electricity. Most of the country is, in theory, connected to the electrical grid, at 69.7 percent.[13] But event those who are connected experience very intermittent access. This is not helpful, if one aims to increase both industrial and domestic productivity. The history of policy-making regarding electrical supply is as confounding as it is scattershot.

Anyone who remembers the 1994 debacle in Kipipiri's by-election, where DP's Mwangi Githiomi won against KANU and – it was rumored – then-president, who postponed his birthday celebrations and poured in state resources, campaigning in person, and *erecting electric high voltage transmission posts* in a promise to the voters that if his candidate, Joe Maina, was elected, there would be electric power all over the constituency. It is rumored that after KANU lost, the electric posts were uprooted and taken away. This is the kind of public policy that makes absolutely no sense.

But Kipipiri was not the exception. Kenyan government's philosophy on electrification was most puzzling. It is with great regret that the author recalls electrical posts reached about 600m away from his residence in 1991. Even then, the whole enterprise around electrical provision was scandalous: two electric power lines, one was HEP and the other Geo-thermal, almost met somewhere near Kirima in Nakuru County.

That this wasn't obvious to those laying the transmission lines was just confounding. Ultimately, electricity was connected in 2019, almost 30 years after it could have ideally been first connected. One considers that the amount of lost income in those thirty years could have changed lives. Even though farmers owned the farms, government would not connect electrical power. Really, it was simple: the government could have connected power on loan, thereby increasing productivity. If the farmer refused to pay the electric charges, they could be disconnected. It is highly doubtful that farmers who own their farms might abscond from a farm to avoid paying bills.

The challenge of electrical blackouts is one that is especially troubling, but this is also tied to the question of how we generate electricity. Power outages are the norm, but they do not have to be. When this candidate lived in the US, the only one time there was a blackout was due to a category 4 storm. It has always been puzzling as to why Kenya almost exclusively uses HEP (and Geothermal to a lesser extent), especially when it is especially well-suited to leverage newer technologies such as solar power to create independent solar grids.

One contends that the issue of power outage and rationing would be somewhat mitigated if both policy (laws) and capacity were changed so that generating electrical power is not the sole preserve of KenGen, that smaller solar power grids can be licensed. As the world cuts down on emissions, this is one of the least expensive changes Kenya can make, which do not have to cost as much as the hypothesized hundreds of billions of dollars.

Potable Water

One of the past policy promises made to Kenya was that by 1999, there would be clean, safe, drinking water flowing into every home. Today, one concludes that either 1999 has not arrived, or that objective was more like pie in the sky. The latter is true. Water remains one of the scarcest commodities in the country, especially clean drinking water. Even in areas with higher levels of rainfall, most Kenyans fetch river water.

This is untenable and unsustainable. Kenya needs to invest – we shall invest – in providing safe, clean, drinking water. Our approach will be premised on the basis that citizens will make good the payments on the bills, otherwise the water can be disconnected. Availing water that is clean and healthy will allow for greater hygiene and access to better quality of life. It will also, in the interim, contribute to an improvement in the economic sector by facilitating use of water to irrigate and grow crops.

But more importantly, it is time to ensure that there is clean, safe, drinking, non-river water within 'acceptable distance' of each home in Kenya, and where possible, inside each home. 'Acceptable distance' is relative; where possible, the 'nyumba kumi' idea is a basis for ensuring clean, safe, drinking water – except with urban housing where ideally, each house should have its own supply of water. We recognize that for areas such as Kibera and other informal settlements, this presents a significant problem, but at minimum, potable water at distance should be one of the government's most immediate concerns.

It is unfathomable that Kenyans still have to fetch water from many kilometers away. We should work to realize this 20-years-overdue goal. This may mean that we build water towers, which can be used to at least supply drinking water. Such water towers exist in many cities, and there is no reason why we cannot do the same for Kenyans.

A Better Infrastructure for the Future
There are some things that we as a nation can do to improve our infrastructure, and to begin to move the country in the direction of progress and modernization more rapidly. For starters, the SGR railway line that now is slated to reach Naivasha should be planned and built to reach Kisumu in the

shortest time possible. A container depot should be built in Kisumu.

This would allow road, rail and water transport of goods into Uganda, Tanzania and onward to Rwanda and Burundi and Eastern DRC. Secondly, it is necessary to revive, and structure, local rail service, even if it will continue to use the existing railway lines. Service from Limuru, Thika and Athi River to Nairobi should be a no-brainer. Third, it is necessary to contemplate the building of light rail, along some of the major public roads, so that Kenya is moving into the future in ways that reflect its importance to itself and the world.

There is need to accelerate the building of highways, but more than anything, a multi-lane highway should be a priority, built between Mombasa, through Nairobi, to Kisumu within 4 years. A northern corridor should be built from Namanga to Moyale, both expanding the Great Northern Highway and being part of the EAC and IGAD RECs road network system. Other major roads should connect major cities and towns in and between the counties.

These will and ought to be managed at the National Government level, but with consultation with the counties. It is important to ensure that paving of roads is durable; but also, that it is using the more modern strategies (for example, some of the most robust roads are using concrete rather than tarmac). It is also important to build express or HOV lanes to ensure that vehicles are not spending more time on the roads when they could get to the city quicker, reduce congestion and emissions. On emissions, it is also important to begin an inspection regime of all motor vehicles.

Laws governing the generation and distribution of electrical power should be changed. The case and outcomes of Telkom make clear that monopolies and state protection of underperforming – indeed in-the-way SEOs is not good for the country. Just as the country has embraced cooperatives as a way to market their products in the farming sector, there is a case to be made for legislation and conditions favoring the creation of electrical producer cooperatives.

Then, individuals and SMEs who can leverage mini-electrical grids that generate renewable energy (perhaps not the windmills that were so controversial), but if an airport in Indianapolis, Indiana, where it snows quite a bit, can generate 30 percent of all its electrical needs from solar, or airports in Arizona generating 100 percent of their electrical needs from solar, there is no law barring the borrowing of good ideas.

Chapter 7: Healthcare, Life Expectancy & Wellness

 GSEOGSEOGSEO

1. Why does Kenya not have a health insurance scheme for the 1.9 million older Kenyans not eligible for coverage by private insurance firms?
2. How can Kenya improve citizen outcomes in health, e.g., in access to healthcare (hospitals), specialized care and other issues related to life expectancy?
3. How effective are new, 'Level X' hospitals in providing care, and do they just have a name or do they have the requisite facilities and services befitting their designation?
4. How can Kenya implement Universal Health Care most equitably and affordably? (Kshs. 6,000 a month won't do)
5. How can HEIs, scientific research institutions and the so-called 'traditional' medicine collaborate to bring about better health outcomes including pharmaceuticals?

Introduction

According to the current government, healthcare in Kenya has seen some improvements. These include the number of NHIF members (6.2 million), an increase in funding (Kshs. 30.75 billion) and the number of social protection beneficiaries (who receive health insurance subsidies, are classified as poor [isn't that half of Kenya], old and disabled) stands at 240,000.[14] This is impressive. But if Kenya actually spends 12 percent of its total annual budgetary expenditures on health allocations (about Kshs. 360 billion out of the Kshs. ~3 trillion budget), it has made strides to improve healthcare. But the numbers hide some of the more significant issues.

It is estimated that about "12.7 percent of sick Kenyans do not seek health care when they are ill with high cost of services being one of the major barriers that accounted for up to 21 percent of those who did not seek care in 2013"[15] while a substantial number risk impoverishment if they seek and are required to pay for healthcare. The cost of healthcare continues to increase, which makes it even more unaffordable. Further, a large chunk of Kenya's population consists of the youth, and while youth are more likely to be healthy, as they build families, the issue of healthcare will continue to occupy them, and concern the national and county governments.

Global and donor cost-sharing requirements have also increased, rising from 5 percent of Kenya's contributions to combat NTDs, Malaria, TB, HIV/AIDS treatments and ARVS increases to 20 percent. But even as donors and development partners require increased cost-sharing especially with health issues, it is necessary to rethink how government allocates funding and prioritize basic services, e.g., health and education.

No particular harm will befall Governors and Ministers if they do not have chase cars; in fact, they are likely moving off and delaying citizens who could use better health care or more proximate hospitals. Without advocating socialism, one wonders whether the expenditure on frills could not be sacrificed in order to allocate more money towards healthcare without upsetting the delicate balance that donors have emphasized. On the other hand, if we just cut graft in the Ministry of Health so that COVID-19 Millionaires are not a thing. Perhaps that kind of money could have been repurposed to combat, for example, respiratory illnesses or Neglected Tropical Diseases.

A substantial number of Kenyans (about 60 percent) work in agriculture, without any formal healthcare benefits, hence the importance of the NHIF. Employer-provided benefits can be important in meeting the cost of healthcare, but even with smaller employers (such as shops and other smaller businesses), these benefits are not offered. Although the government wants to collect revenue, it is useful to consider whether there is a need to offset employer cost of providing healthcare with taxes.

It may reduce the revenues generated, but will no doubt increase the overall subscription to NHIF. It is also necessary to encourage farmers and other small-scale concerns to invest in healthcare benefits. One estimates that without a steady source of income (farming can be very...unpredictable) and thus, most Kenyan farmers are likely to forego healthcare out of fear that they would be wasting money.

Hospitals and Healthcare Facilities

On any given day, at any hospital with a semblance of a decent reputation, tens, even hundreds of Kenyans queue up to access healthcare services. For the most part, these are Kenyans who are at the point of pain or other severe disease manifestation. Patients with various types of maladies are made to queue, sit, wait or be right next to each other. This brooks the question of whether hospital practices do indeed spread more contagion even as they seek to heal those who seek health services.

Perhaps the hospitals know that maybe the illnesses are not contagious, but one might equally chalk up these practices to the lack of knowledge, consideration, space, or all of these. Just because our fellow citizens are unwell is no reason to infect them with other conditions while they wait for treatment, because then that makes recovery more challenging. There is a need to review how we provide care, so that hospitals are not places that we dread to go to, but places in which healing can take place.

With devolved government, there has been a sudden explosion in the number of especially hospitals now labeled 'Level 5', indicating that they are some of the best healthcare facilities in the county and possibly country. However, some of the hospitals just slapped on the 'Level 5' label but had no significant expansion in space, services or capacity.

It is wonderful to have many hospitals – although the need for many hospitals might speak to our overall state of health. But it is even better to have hospitals that provide quality healthcare. While devolution did bring health services closer to the citizens, not all hospitals are equally equipped. It is necessary for the government to elevate a few select hospitals to perhaps Level 6, which would receive referrals from Level 5 Hospitals. But it is also important to have a culture of health, not just sickness.

Training, Ethics Qualifications and Quacks

It is especially important to ensure the proper training for doctors, nurses and other healthcare professionals, for peoples' lives depend on it. In the past two decades, it has been the case that all manner of quacks have set up shop and proclaimed themselves to be healers. A medical practitioner in Engineer, who calls himself Dr. K, is a former Licensed Practical Nurse (LPN) whose license was pulled by the Commonwealth of Massachusetts after his working in nursing home there. It is not clear why the license was pulled, but one suspects that it was not for giving candy to his patients or for showing great care.

There are many other cases of individuals setting up shop, calling themselves doctors and dispensing medication, even though their qualifications are suspect. YouTube also has ample evidence of wrongdoing by Kenyan medics, including that one doctor who would rape his patients under anesthesia. Yet, there is no record of any serious, sustained and ongoing vetting being done by the responsible accreditation bodies so as to uncover these quacks, or ensuring that this is not a one-off occurrence, particularly in the context of such an important issue.

As a country and government, we need to — we pledge to ensure that training of the medical professionals and paraprofessionals is of the highest caliber. Ethics within the medical profession need to be Hippocratic, and more closely monitored. Just as city and county inspectorates frequent the various businesses, it is necessary that only the properly trained and qualified provide medical care, and with consistent oversight of their practice and ongoing training to ensure best practices.

All quacks have to be excluded and properly prosecuted. But the government also needs to be more efficient at both remunerating the medical providers and assuring that their working conditions are favorable and comparable to other regions of the world, to avoid the brain drain that especially targets them. The frequent sight of doctors, nurses and pharmacists on the streets is immensely troubling, for the strikes lead to many deaths, as has been evident in the past.

Health Insurance and Discrimination of the Elderly

The National Hospital Insurance Fund (NHIF) is an important path to funding healthcare in Kenya. Whereas the proposals for strengthening and funding healthcare access through both the NHIF and UHC are outlined elsewhere, it is important to address health insurance, its affordability, and the discrimination that is inherent in the current health insurance system.

The latter is especially significant: most healthcare providers will not insure anyone over 65 years of age, and will often drop them in the event that they turn 65. This is one of the absolutely worst possible practices the government has allowed. When you are 65 and older, you are likely to have more health challenges, be less able to perform work in order to make money with which they might pay for medical care.

The government already recognized some of the shortfalls experienced by senior citizens, when it implemented the Older Persons Cash Transfer (OPCT) or Inua Jamii cash transfer program. If the elderly do not have the economic means to support themselves, what makes us believe that they have the capacity to pay for healthcare out of pocket, considering their exclusion from purchasing private health insurance?

The number of the elderly who would potentially be covered by any private health insurance is also relatively small. According to current government statistics, about 240,000 elderly and indigent persons are receiving some sort of funding from the government This varies from the monthly Kshs. 2,000 payment that is often conflated with the every-four-months-Inua Jamii Senior Citizens' scheme that was slated for September 2020.[16]

Although healthcare, particularly its funding and whether it is a basic human right, continues to divide opinion even in the most developed countries, there are values that a nation can hold, and decide what is important to them. Kenya aspires to enact a Universal Health Care (UHC) program, which has been articulated as one of the four pillars (or the Big Four) of the outgoing government. UHC and improved health are expected to lead to the achievement of Agenda 2030 and meet the recommendations of the AU's 2001 Abuja Declaration[17] to spend at least 15% of their budget on healthcare financing..

It is nigh impossible to achieve any of a nation's goals without a healthy, robust workforce, and it is also not possible to arrive at that destination by discriminating part of the citizenry. Broadly, healthcare can be made more efficient, affordable, but also, a priority of the next government. But often, the devil is in the details: how to fund UHC, and the quality of universal health care. For there is a difference between universal healthcare and actually healthcare that improves the quality of life and doesn't merely suppress disease.

There is no doubt that accessible, affordable, universal health care is not only in the interest of Kenya – sickness is expensive, decreases productivity and costs the nation many lost hours – it is also one of the most central functions of government. Leaving healthcare to the market is short-sighted, as the current pandemic has shown us. Healthcare is also a human right, and a foundational principle of government under the idea of 'wellbeing' (or common welfare). The cost of healthcare in Kenya is astronomical, and has to be reduced proactively and reactively.

Proactively, by emphasizing on health screenings, better nutrition, scientific-based decisions on health (e.g., immunization), and active government involvement in developing positive healthcare policies that are not just responsive to the incidence of sickness; reactively by encouraging individuals to seek health care even in challenging times such as the current pandemic. We must not only target the healthy and well-to-do; we must also exercise our social and 'African' responsibility to our parents and grandparents, the older generation.

Healthcare Philosophy, Holistic and Traditional Medicine

Kenyans go to hospital when they are sick. This is a well-established practice, and a most regrettable reality, one borne of the most persistent attitudes regarding wellness and illness as some sort of weakness. Health and healthcare do not entail just going to hospital to receive treatment when one is unwell. There is a holistic approach to thinking about and *doing* health. It also includes working hard to be healthy, and preventing some of the reasons for the most challenging future doctor visits.

Issues such as screening for the different cancers, diabetes, high blood pressure and other common diseases and health complications ought to be part of our healthcare philosophy. After all, did we not borrow that very British statement, that 'prevention is better than cure'? Preventing hospitalization will also allow the healthcare system to be more efficient and give better care. But there is also a place for promoting and embracing more holistic healing, not just through medication.

We need to also acknowledge that there is a health care industry that exists just below the formal hospital care system. It is almost informal, but it also has the promise of being more than just old men dishing out vines and herbs and roots whose medical benefits might be suspect. How many of us are familiar with such resources as *Muarubaini, thabai,* blue gum tree leaves (boiled), *Wanjiru wa rurii, munua nugu,* ginger, garlic, lemons, limes and a hundred other potential traditional cures?

Rather unfortunately, in our transition from the traditional societies that predated this current modernity, we have allowed or knowledge of these to begin to lapse, even as they have appeared to enjoy a resurgence and effectiveness hitherto not thought possible. We ought not allow knowledge that was often borne of experience to laps. We must also embrace the notion of holistic medicine, moving it from an after-thought or the domain of old men long past their time, to making it central to our current realities and having these supplement our current, 'western' healthcare and pharmaceutical systems.

This is the function of both medical research and community research. If there is any value to any of these products, and others not highlighted here, we ought to capture that value before those who are knowledgeable can no longer educate us as to these resources. Besides, there is value to either confirming or disconfirming the benefits these products bring. Although Madagascar has been laughed out of COVID-19 town, most Kenyans know someone who has likely caught COVID-19, and used a combination of traditional herbs and cures *and* seemed to come out on the other side with nary a problem. Perhaps there is some value to investigating these resources.

On Mental Health

One of the most overlooked issues in the health and well-being of Kenyans is the issue of mental health, or mental wellness. Over the past two years especially, with the pandemic raging and its attendant outcomes, such as quarantine and an overall increase in the amount of stress, including by both students and parents, the issue of mental health had risen to the fore.

How we as Kenyans deal with mental health is most intriguing – and not in a positive way. Most communities have just one description of mental health challenges: "madness." This is such a 17th century approach, that we urgently need to update our approaches to our thinking about mental health, but also to engage in an educational campaign thereof. Mental health is a medical issue, rather than a traditions-based issue. We need to bring it into the medical realm, and consider how to deal with it without the shame and stigma associated with mental health.

It is estimated that about 20 percent of Kenya's population deals with some diagnosis of a mental illness, even though these are not necessarily yet diagnosed. This statistic tracks with the global averages (for example, in the US, about 25 percent of the population is estimated to be diagnosed with and – or – living with mental illness). For Kenya, this comes to about 11 million persons. "Mad" is not a definition of any sort. The 1505-page, 5th Edition of the Diagnostic and Statistical Manual of Mental Disorders (DSM-5) explains types of disorders.

In particular, DSM-5 highlights the 22 classes of disorders, further subdivided into another several hundred disorders. Today, Kenya has insufficient numbers of properly trained mental health providers, from psychiatrists to counselors, and it is time to correct this anomaly. If other countries have about 25 percent of populations needing mental health care, Kenya is not vastly different. The events of the past few years have shown us that it is an issue we cannot and should not ignore any longer.

The Future

We aim to set national priorities and **must-fund, non-discretionary healthcare spending**. In doing so, we will be borrowing a (good) leaf from the major economies and developed countries, with spending on such issues as defense, Medicaid, Medicare or Great Britain's National Health Service. Other partners such as Nordic states and most of Europe have some element of subsidized healthcare; other issues might be less important, but healthcare is not one of them.

We pledge to vociferously make the case that poor health is a global issue, as has been seen with the COVID-19 pandemic; not funding or providing vaccines impacts the rest of the world, and considering that new diseases and pandemics are likely to continue emerging, it is necessary to increase healthcare spending and cover most Kenyans. *This is good business, even for donor nations.* It might require cutting down on such expenditure as County Governors' chase cars, personal body-guards and security at their homes, but healthcare is a basic need and right.

It is necessary to eliminate, forthwith, the discrimination that the elderly face, in attempting to access private health insurance. **Healthcare discrimination** by private firms against the elderly is against our ethos as Africans. And even where the private healthcare industry fails to take quick action, the government should, and will, extend the leaf it borrowed from progressive nations when it implemented the Older Persons Cash Transfer (OPCT) program: either pay for NHIF for all over-65s, or create a Medicare-like program that funds healthcare for the elderly.

The former is actually probably more feasible: after all, estimates suggest that a mere 2.92 percent of the country is aged 65 and over. And considering that life expectancy is around 68 years, it probably wouldn't break the government to pay for health insurance for 1.4 million seniors. In addition to this, we aim to require that any private health insurer doing business in Kenya must insure at least a percentage of seniors over 65, commensurate with their market share of the health market.

One cannot just hope that people will do the right thing (after all, they have not been doing it, or else government may be unnecessary. Those insurers opting out of insuring the corresponding percentage of seniors would then be penalized, funds of which will be used by the government to fund healthcare for seniors >65. In principle, we must also end the discrimination that treats the elderly as less-than Kenyan. Even if it makes good business sense, excluding the elderly from private health insurance markets is simply unconscionable.

There is no monopoly on good ideas, and while the **Universal Health Care** (UHC) proposal has not been fully implemented, our future administration aims to extend coverage by NHIF at current levels to all Kenyans, whether on the basis of coverage under a family unit, or as employer-paid contributions for those in formal employment. The recent proposal, debated by the National Assembly to increase the cost of NHIF contributions to Kshs. 6,000 per member, however, is especially ill-advised. If Kenya's per capita GDP is US$1,400 (about Kshs. 140,000 a year), asking an individual to spend Kshs. 72,000 per year, over 51.5 percent of their income on a health insurance scheme is especially naïve or it disregards the current realities of Kenyans' state of wealth.

Future governments must commit, and we do, to fulfilling immediately, the commitments of the Abuja declaration of allocating 15 percent of **government expenditure to health**. But even the 15 percent suggested is quite low. Government should and will identify those critical areas where its major investments should go, and while the Big Four might include manufacturing and health care, it is necessary to also invest in education and security as basic services. More critical will be the process to identify what is actually indispensable and the issues upon which the nation's fortunes rise and fall.

With regard to **detaining indigent patients in hospitals**, the government must, and will commit to eradicating the policies and practices of healthcare facilities and providers of detaining Kenyans who have an outstanding hospital bill, until such a bill is paid. There is all kinds of wrongs with this approach. For starters, one wants to believe that health is one of the most important issues, so no one will refuse to pay hospital bills if they are going to get better and regain their health.

But sickness is inherently debilitating. It makes absolutely no sense to detain someone because they are not able to pay, and at the same time, their prolonged presence in the facility moves it no closer to payment of outstanding bills, but also *increases* what they need to pay in future. It is not clear what system needs to be in place (proof of places of residence, recorded ID details, payment plans...) but detaining indigent patients is morally wrong and dehumanizing.

A future administration needs to **comprehensively address mental health wellness**, including the sensitization of the public regarding mental health. It is especially important to confront the stigmas and erroneous beliefs that suggest that mental illness somehow stems from being 'bewitched,' being possessed by evil spirits or being cursed. We have to be proactive and educate our people that mental health has nothing to do with our socio-cultural traditions or violation thereof, and that they exist in other countries with dissimilar beliefs and traditions.

We also need to educate providers and the public as to how to better care for individuals diagnosed with the spectrum of mental illnesses. Advanced nations have progressively moved to de-institutionalize those living with mental illnesses, equipping them with the skills, knowledge and abilities to function **within community settings.** This also calls for training of mental health care specialists who will work with these individuals to improve their ADL skills. But there is an even bigger task, that of destigmatizing mental health and illness, providing greater understanding and providing better care than asking families to deal with it.

It is also essential to pursue a **holistic approach to healthcare and wellness.** We need to put in place strategies where public-private partnerships work together to increase health screenings, health clinics and open community health forums that include Q & A on the most pertinent health issues, including screenings for such conditions as diabetes, high blood pressure and other non-stigmatizing illnesses.

We need to move Kenyans from a culture of only going to hospital when they are unwell, to one of being proactive about their health, including through better nutrition. Checkups and open, free clinics are also likely to catch some of these medical issues before they require hospitalization, while it will also create a culture of health and wellness-mindedness, rather than the culture of sickness and fear of health that we seem to embrace now.

This campaign believes that it is especially important to strengthen the existing hospitals and other similar facilities around the country. While Level 5 hospitals are especially important, we believe that further **designating Level 6 hospitals** (of course after suitably equipping) with all the important facilities and relevant personnel, so that they will carry out the specialized services like heart surgeries, separation of conjoined babies, Proton Therapy treatments and other similarly elevated levels of specialist care is important. This negates need to travel abroad for specialist care.

We further propose that a Level 6 hospital each be located within each group of counties (based on the former provinces), so as to both provide proximate health care services that are of the highest quality. This will also cut down on the cost of seeking treatment outside the country and in the near future, provide similar services to countries in the region.

Our universities are engaged in high level research. Now we must move them in the direction of researching and developing new treatments for illnesses especially those localized to the region. It is important to strengthen the **universities' research capacity in healthcare** especially in the areas of STEM, but also in healthcare. Improving our capacity for diagnosing those illnesses that afflict our citizens will be important, relevant and avoid the 'Henrietta Lacks' problem, and more broadly, the issue of most health research and products used in Kenya and Africa being made for and by the west.

We celebrate the recent discovery of a malaria vaccine, but believe that this is only the start. Much funding and expertise exists, which can be used to create joint research programs with universities in the country and with collaboration with other institutions. Funding enables local research capacity-building and stems brain drain, thus enabling the country to become a research hub. Despite the global reaction to South Africa having success in sequencing the Omicron variant of the COVID-19 virus, there are other areas where we can make progress and solve healthcare challenges within the country and region without experiencing detrimental blowbacks.

An example of medical research funding collaborations and opportunities stems from the Bill and Melinda Gates Foundation. However, we should not just depend on largesse to develop research capacities. Research leads to discovery of **new medications, developing and strengthening pharmaceutical production**. Further, the research must include traditional healers, for it is clear that there are local sources of expertise that we have not always leveraged.

Some of the research will be directed at harnessing local cures so that we are less dependent on western pharma, and bleeding billions for things we can manufacture. It will also allow for the development of pharmaceuticals relevant to the entire region. Pharmaceutical exports are especially valuable, and if we can create a pharmaceutical export base, we stand to not only improve our healthcare services, but also fund them without resorting to begging donors to help the country with meeting its increasingly complex healthcare needs.

We intend to train and develop community-level healthcare workers, to be known as **Community Healthcare Specialists**. These will be funded and engaged jointly by the National Government and by the County Governments. CHS's will be empowered to provide basic health services that do not require specialist care, such as nutritional guidance, testing services (e.g., for diabetes, high blood pressure, etc.) and possibly referral services.

During the proposed community health fairs, such CHS's will be able to do such screenings, provide basic services such as blood drawings, referrals to major health providers in the event of serious illness or suspicion thereof, and other health care advice such as proper nutrition and diet. Their work will allow for a low-cost service that also reduces the overcrowding seen in hospitals, allowing for more time to provide better care. This also allows for a better and healthier community so that we move from the idea of sick care to healthcare.

The government will also need to deal with the issue of drug use and abuse, which has been on the rise both in schools and in society in general. There is also greater need to deal with the so-called 'gateway drugs,' the low-level, entry-type of drugs such as marijuana, which are by law outlawed. Whether government deals with that other source of income for some parts of the Central Kenya region, *miraa* and *muguka*, is a more political question. One considers that this would be a highly charged issue, and the likelihood of banning it is dim at best.

The government, and by extension, society, needs to recognize and educate the public that contrary to what was the case in advanced industrial countries, drug use and abuse is not just a criminal issue; it is also an addiction issue. Notwithstanding, it is evident, and necessary, that the drug dealers and suppliers should be arrested, prosecuted, jailed and the keys probably thrown into the ocean. Drug use and abuse is especially a health issue, and we ought to have learnt from the situation with 'glue.'

There is an urgent need to invest in **drug treatment and rehabilitation facilities**, in training rehabilitation professionals, in therapy, counseling and other mitigation strategies to address the issue. It is especially important to nip this issue in the bud, by not only because the consequences of drug use and abuse are especially costly in the end, but also because the youth are the future and if the drug problems continue, there will be an entire wasted generation. This is one of those instances where we need to learn from the example of others.

Chapter 8: Education and Educational outcomes

號ঝেঝেঝে

1. Why do we countenance an education system that 'fail's 90 percent of the pupils who join Std. 1 as they matriculate into tertiary education (university, colleges, etc.?)
2. What is wrong (if anything is) with the new CBC (and how can what's wrong be fixed?)
3. Is Kenya's education system fundamentally flawed, as originally designed by the British to produce 'workers' rather than employees, and how can we change this?
4. How can we separate education from examination, so that we foster a culture of discovery, innovation, creativity and use of technologies more modern than chalk and boards?

Introduction

Successive iterations of Kenya's education system, from 7-4-2-3 to 8-4-4 to the current, if much aligned and contentious CBC, or Competency-Based Curriculum, often evoke the image of a stone house built on sand. And not just sand, *quicksand*. One can add bricks, try to shore it up, attempt to right the corner-posts, add a paved floor and decorate it, remove the *makuti* and replace with Galsheet, but beneath the edifice, the fundamental structure, the foundation, is unsound.

Kenya's education system was first authored by the British; all we have done to it is tweaking it here and there. It is necessary to question why the British inaugurated the education system bequeathed unto Kenya: the goal was to educate what was considered inferior but compliant, non-thinking, unimaginative, yes-sir type of 'workers' for the empire.

The system was not designed to educate inquisitive minds: creators, inventors, patent-holders, or great scientists who would go on to challenge the very ideas taught by successive systems. Did Livingstone really discover Victoria Falls? The falls had been there since creation or evolution. Did the Portuguese become the first Europeans to sail around Africa? They may have, but China's Zheng He's voyages were bigger and better financed. These are the fundamentals of a system that informs of the past, but does not design a future, the future of Kenya and East Africa and more broadly, the African continent.

Kenya and Africa have perfected the art of tweaking the various things that were largely designed in Europe, even if they were made for Africa. Countries, rather than starting from scratch, take taking stuff Europeans created, frequently, if not mostly out of ignorance or the need for oppression of the locals and decidedly, their miseducation (African nations borders are a case in point) and attempt to make it work. So it is with our education system. With every tweak, we congratulate ourselves for a job well done, even if it is absolutely shoddy and the outcomes are less than optimal.

We never stop to ask ourselves the most basic, fundamental question(s): what is the objective of our educational system as it is currently structured? Is it to dissuade young people as to their intellectual capacities, or is it to prepare them for the future of a globalized world, a world of communications, internet, travel and that is globally interconnected? If it is the latter, the system does an E-level job. The other explanations is that Kenya, as with most African governments, know that post-European stuff including the educational systems are flawed, but are either too lazy to change them, or that they serve a purpose similar to what they did under European colonization: keeping the populace uninformed and pliant. Nothing, they say, is more dangerous than a well-educated people.

Educational technology use

Kenya's educational system's outcomes are as predictable as they are sub-optimal. Education content delivery is also highly antiquated, relying on anywhere from up to fifty to sixty pupils crammed in a room next to each other like sardines, sitting on those old, wooden forms and desks, most of the teachers predictably using a chalkboard, few instructional aids except things like maps and letter charts.

In this context, todays pupils, who live in the age of technology, and of whom some own various forms of technology such as phones and tablets, are literally taught the same way and with the same 'technology' as their great grandparents would have used. The only change that has occurred in the primary school I last attended more than 30 years ago is the addition of an electrical outlet. There are not even electric bulbs. Clearly, the technology in use then, is still in use today. Essentially, Kenyan schools have continued using 17th Century technology to prepare students for the 22nd century.

In the meantime, since I last sat at that desk, the world invented the personal computer (PC), a.k.a. the laptop, internet, Windows, Microsoft Office software, cell phones, social media, especially YouTube, Learning Management Systems (LMSs) such as Blackboard, overhead projectors, LCD projectors, mounted LCD Activ[R] panels in classrooms, smart boards and other types of instructional technology, which could take advantage of the trillions of bytes of free content on the internet.

Additionally, in violation of every student's educational privacy, we cheerfully post grades on the notice-board outside, displaying and likely subsequently heightening every student's shame, especially if they do not perform well. We still use chalk and the chalkboard; we haven't even moved to the lesser technology of dry-erase boards. This brings us to that mind-boggling 2013 presidential election and its promises.

Then, there was a still-born promise to equip each Grade 1 (standard 1) pupil with a tablet. As promises and plans go, this is absolutely the worst possible educational public policy and plan to equip pupils with any instructional type of technology. For starters, somewhere before the mid-course of the 12-year primary-to-secondary school transition, the country would have to replace the tablets, unless use of old technology is our thing (and considering chalk-boards and chalk, it clearly is). Technology is changing at warp speed, and it is not clear if very outdated technology is better or worse than none.

Consider this: Facebook was not exactly a household name in 2008, even though it had existed, ever since Mark's Harvard dorm room, since 2004. YouTube, although three years old in 2008, had not started hosting such monumental video content or hosting channels such as Crash Course World History, which can teach learners so much content within 10 minutes it is fascinating to watch. Instagram and WhatsApp were also not household names, even though today they are all the rage. It is estimated that technology doubles every two years.

To equip first grade pupils with a tablet means that the technology will likely have changed 6 times before they get ready to enter the formal employment market. Further, 500,000 of them will have dropped out along the way, and it is not clear what utility a Std. 8 drop-out (or deferred educational opportunity) person can do with that 8-year old tablet, particularly if they end up being farmers, given the job conditions and skills level. Conversely, if you equipped Form 3 and 4 students with the devices, they will enter the workforce (or higher education) within the technology life cycle and therefore will not be using 12-year old technology when they graduate.

Educational Transitions and Miseducation of Kenyan Youth

In January 2003, with the new NARC government taking power, more than 1 million new pupils joined school, some for the first time. The most memorable of these was Mzee Kimani Maruge, 84, whose picture sitting next to children four generations removed from his captured the importance of education, but also, the imagination of the whole world, and later culminated in his address to the United Nations, one for which my jealousy – but recognition – was stoked.

In 2011, almost a million of the same group of students sat for the KCPE exam. Of these, almost half a million would be deemed to have 'passed,' but crucially, the other half simply did disappear from the educational system. *Forever.* In 2014, the 'surviving' near-half million sat for the KCSE national exam. From among these, almost 100,000 would gain places in the several public and private universities, TTCs and the major national polytechnics. They were to be congratulated heartily: they had survived 12 years of the meat-grinder that has been the Kenyan education system.

What became of the rest? In 2011 (or February, 2012), the country sat by and watched half a million – yes, 500,000 kids, pupils, drop out of the formal education system, with nary a comment. What was to become of them? What do they become and how do their lives end up? After KCPE, most of the 'unsuccessful' are usually about 14, clearly too young for the formal employment market, possess no national ID (at that age, they are clearly under-age); thus, they are both less educated, under-age and unemployable. They cannot possibly obtain any business loans, do not own property, or even own independent residential situation But this is not an isolated event or limited to 2012. It is as perennial as Christmas, and as a nation, we've let it go on for eternity. That is a blot on us collectively.

The Kenyan education system has perfected the art of dropping, and basically killing the dreams of half a million pupils each year, denying them the opportunity to continue on the one path that has often been the one sure path to future job opportunities. *Each Year.* If you consider just the past two decades, this comes to a whooping ten million pupils whom we have not educated past 8th grade, or equipped with skills other than farming.

Granted, dropping out of 8th grade (Std. 8) is not a death knell: these citizens (almost) they can go on to become successful farmers, or bicycle / motorcycle repair persons, but is this how as a country we get to a Low to Medium Income Country? Yet even with these depressing numbers, even being part of the 10 percent who transition from pre-school to tertiary education does not give much of a guarantee for a job in an economy with up to 40 percent unemployment.

If the half a million pupils who make it to secondary school is a celebratory number, four years later brings untold misery, as another 400,0000 are dropped after the KCSE. This group is much more educated. They can tell you that a spider is in the Animal Kingdom, and that it is an arachnid. How useful that information is, is still to be contemplated. But over each 12-year period, with ruthless efficiency, the Kenyan education system accepts almost 1 million pupils in Standard 1 (or future Grade 1), and enrolls 100,000 in tertiary education.

It is not clear that secondary school education is sufficient to give the 'unsuccessful' the necessary skills to navigate life: math, English, Swahili, biology, chemistry and physics, history and CRE (religion) are hardly life-skills at 14, neither are they at age 18. Not all pupils take business studies, and even when they do, it is estimated that in many countries, over 90% of all new businesses fail, unless the business they are into is one of raising rabbits. How this has not bothered our policy-makers is beyond comprehension. On the other hand, most of those who run government and education are elites, whose children do not have to necessarily contend with such 'inconveniences.'

As a country, we have accepted that Kenya's education system produces 90% 'failures,' and is therefore, arguably, designed to produce failures. Our youth are educated through a system designed, but subsequently mangled and tortured to produce half-'workers' and 'employees,' not creators, thinkers or inventors. It is not clear that for all his genius, Einstein would have found the key to $E=MC^2$ if he were educated in Kenya.

It is time to restructure our education system so that it focuses less on the fact that a spider is an 8-legged arachnid, knowledge that is perfectly useless for a form four non-university-attending Kenyan, and focus on skills, knowledge and aptitude that are useful to proceed to acquire tertiary education, but to also be creators and inventors.

Our education system needs to invest in the teachers and instructors being well educated so that they, and the education system, can prepare students for the future. Further, we need to build such alternatives that there is sufficient continuity, so that interruptions do not become a lifelong sentence into a lack of educational achievement. And it is also time to make education truly free of cost, notwithstanding what the IFIs suggest.

Proposals for a Better Education in Kenya: *Free Education*

Almost-free, Free Primary Education is not good enough, and it most certainly is insufficient to help Kenyans lead better lives. Those who drop out before secondary or tertiary level are barely equipped for the future technological world. Although basic literacy is important, it is mostly unlikely to lead to the kind of significant finds and innovations that can rival the Apples and Googles, Facebooks and Twitters of this world (with apologies to Safaricom and MPESA). There is no better way to build the human resources Kenya needs than education, or at least, by ensuring that there is a parallel utilitarian technical education. And making education free is not only good, it is *necessary.*

We pledge to make education in all primary schools and day secondary schools free of cost, fully funded by the government. Boarding schools will only be allowed to charge market-rate 'boarding fee' to provide for food and accommodation. We will guarantee every child in Kenya 12 years free education and have 100% transition from primary to secondary to tertiary education. Equivalency education will also be free (GED) up to 12th grade equivalent. A free, quality, technology-informed education is one of our pledges to make a Better Educated Kenya.

Technology

The use of technology in instruction, in the information age, is not a choice — it cannot be. Unless we as Kenyans utilize technology as part of, and to deliver the curriculum, to instruct our students, we fail to take advantage of all the materials available for free that would change educational experiences and achievements. We also fail to equip our students with the most contemporary, up-to-date technology and ways in which the world communicates information – we should not be aspiring to be left in the smoke-and-talking-drums era.

Besides equipping future Kenyan citizens with information and technology, we have to give them the ability to compete, and an opportunity to take advantage of the existing resources. The amount of information available is said to double every two years, yet we make no provision to make this available to learners even though they have access to smartphones at home. This, of course, requires providing said technology – computers, projectors, cheap, affordable internet access and God forbid, a stable, reliable electrical supply. The latter can be achieved through mini-grids that utilize solar power.

Globally, there have been collaborations between tech firms and learning institutions. We do frequently hear of millions of dollars' grants, and government cannot just depend on largesse. Yet an all-of-the-above strategy is needed. Working with firms such as Alphabet and their floating internet, and other educational technology companies also offers the opportunity to demonstrate the utility of such approaches and programs. Of course, equipping all 10,000 primary schools and an almost equal number of secondary schools will be a challenge.

A more feasible approach would be to equip, for starters, each secondary school, at least the form 3 and form 4 classes, with at least a projector and laptop, three if possible, so that the teachers can design learner experiences for this century, and thus improve their educational experience.

Enough free content exists already, free and available to all, and there is no need for a teacher to torture the imagination of their pupils to conceptualize a swimming jelly fish while you can see that on a YouTube video. It is time to use 21st technology to teach millennials. Within three years, we shall equip every secondary school in Kenya with at minimum a laptop, an LCD projector and one printer at a cost of Kshs. 540 million.

Educational achievement: Exam-based Education Systems
There is a correlation between number of patents filed and the type of educational system in place. Even more advanced nations such as China, which rely on an exam-based educational system, fail to procure creativity in their students. Our system is one of rote-learning, requiring recall, memorization, rather than application. So, what if a spider is an arachnid? Or a fern is a lichen (not sure it is)? This is knowledge that would have utility to a future biologist, but for an average Kenyan, not so much.

Our educational system has to move away from rote-learning and exams, and emphasize application, creativity (and not just creating or making clay pots). Within five years, Kenya will have teams that will compete at global events such as the global robotics competitions (even the failed state that is Afghanistan can manage to do that). In consultation with a broad swathe of stakeholders, we will reform the educational system to reduce 'failure' and ensure the system focuses on more 'application' rather than rote-learning. This is our contract for *A Better Educated Kenya.*

Continuing education
No matter where an individual's education becomes 'temporarily' interrupted, they should be able to, and have the opportunity, to resume, and complete whichever level of

education they desire. At the present time, this is not the case in Kenya. Global research has demonstrably shown that education has many more – and just as often, lifelong – benefits than just getting a job: benefits that even contribute to a healthier nation.

For "as we have learned, educated women have fewer children, educate their children, and are more self-sufficient, protect the environment, and benefit the economy. The quality of community life is dramatically related to the education of women and girls."[18] As a country, Kenya are better off with more educated citizens, be they girls or boys, the latter more likely to support in gender equality. Education need not be a be-all, end-all, and any interruption should not be a sentence into future inability to graduate, unto the never-graduated-or-continued-with-school.

With truly free education at all levels, anyone will be able to resume their educational journey without going into a classroom as the current system operates. This requires certifying educational centers that can do residential and online learning, in modules. An example of this exists, with the US General Equivalency Diploma (G.E.D.) which tests at the high school level, often one subject at a time, all subject exams completed within a year or any other stipulated period.

For those who so intend, joining university under self, or private sponsorship, or through educational loans, should be a lifelong opportunity, rather than restricted to a specific year as the current KUCCPS and the previous JAB facilitated. It is our promise to make a better educated Kenya, a Kenya with lifelong opportunity to complete high school by obtaining a GED (equivalent) by providing opportunities

Educational exchanges

We pledge that the Ministry of Education will offer opportunities for the best performing public students to go on education exchanges in other countries, providing them with exposure to other cultures and education systems. Besides the ordinary functions, we pledge to form an office of Global Programs.

It will coordinate these foreign students' studies and activities. There is no reason Kenyan students are not participating in Yale Educational Exchanges, among others. Global perspectives do inform future Kenyan citizens and create a more tolerable world. In addition, taking advantage of those widely available scholarships and sponsorships increases the citizenry to which the country can turn especially when such labor export arrangements as proposed here are implemented.

Educational rights and privacy
Remember that time in 2017 when Kenyans *demanded* that Amherst College 'release' Uhuru Kenyatta's undergraduate degree certificate and the response was 'crickets'? That was because of the US federal law titled the Family Educational Rights and Privacy Act (FERPA). The law prohibits the release of an/any individual's educational records without authorization from their owner, unless they waive the right, usually by signing a document to that effect. The issue of private information – educational or health – is protected, because it can be used for many nefarious reasons. There is a companion, US law governing health records, the Health Insurance Portability and Accountability Act of 1996 (HIPAA). Kenya has a version of it, for especially for health information.

In our contract with, and for *A Better Educated Kenya* – we propose that all educational records be treated as personal and protected information that should not be shared with the public or with others who have little, if any, public interest to access that information. For this purpose, we pledge to eradicate the rampant display of students' grades on notice-boards in schools, as is currently done with examination grades.

Besides the lack of consent to share the grades, poor performance displayed for all to see is a shaming device which can have a negative impact on a student. If requested by the proper authorities for legitimate use and goals, e.g., verification by employers, colleges, IEBC or other government agencies, educational records can be shared and/or accessed.. Educational records are personal records. Just as we do not share the health and banking and ID information, we'll privatize individuals' educational information.

Chapter 9: Youth, Future and/as Human Resources

෬෩෬෩෬෩

1. What is Kenya's national strategy for youth (almost 37 million of Kenyans aged 34 and below)? Is there a national strategy and if not, can a nation ignore 37 million citizens and their needs?
2. Why and how are Kenya's youth (under)represented in structures of authority and what is the most optimal way to ensure their representation?
3. How can the executive implement strategies to assure that each cabinet department, the civil service and even County Governments focus on youth in development?
4. How do Kenyan youths perceive their position in the nation? What are their hopes but especially frustrations? How can youth help build the future of their country?

Introduction

"Kenya is a very youthful country," declares the opening lines of an OHCHR publication by Odondi. Although the numbers in this particular publication do not exactly cover youth years as defined by the United Nations (the UN considers youth to be individuals between 15 and 24 years of age), they illuminate just how youthful Kenya indeed is. Kenya's total population that is aged between zero and 14 is almost 41 percent, at 18 million. Those aged 15-24 are 18.83 percent of the population, or close to 9 million Kenyans.

Together, Kenyans who are aged 0-25 account for close to a healthy 60 percent of Kenya's population.[19] Other sources are more discerning. For example, Ndungu estimates that as of the 2019 Population and Census results, 75 percent of 47.6 million is under 35 years of age – bringing that number to about 37 million in raw population, while the elderly – over 65 years of age – population is 1.87 million.[20]

While Ndungu's numbers refer to 2019, the year of the national population census, a UK Research Briefing Note from 2015 already found that the population then stood at 47 million. On the other hand, Baraza finds that 75 percent of Kenya's population is aged below 35, and makes further distinctions to cover the official 'youth' category: ~14 million.[21]

A bit of creative math results in a computed total population of 18.5 million Kenyans aged between 15 and 34.[22] Current numbers suggest that Kenya's population has significantly grown since these numbers were first published; it is common to estimate that the current population is anywhere between 53 million and 55 million. CIA World Factbook's estimate puts the population at 54.68 million in July 2021, and the total population between 0-24 years at 31.67 million, or 59.16 percent of the total population.[23] By extrapolation, one might conclude that the *total* population is in the region of 55 million.

Who the youth are is often a shifting target depending on the source of the definition. The UN considers youth to be aged between 15 and 24,[24] a somewhat narrow window. The East African Community considers those aged 15-35, while Kenya's 2010 Constitution defined youth as aged 18-31, changing from a previous National Youth Policy that had the minimum age at 15 and the maximum at 30.[25] Notwithstanding, one concludes that there are *many* young people in Kenya. A lot.

Thus, although the young citizens will someday grow into being the youth in the definition of what constitutes the youth, ages 15 to 35, it helps to focus on the current numbers, but with appreciation of the current and future policies that must account for this future growth in the youth numbers. Further, if the current trends hold, with a population estimated at 115 million by 2060, it will be important to ensure that the youth are at the forefront of any planning the country does.

It is commendable, that the current government has a Youth Enterprise Development Fund, complete with a national strategy that appeals to all the relevant development goals and targets: The Big Four, Vision 2030, the UN's Sustainable Development Goals and Africa's Vision 2063. At the same time, it is clear that while youth affairs are widely covered by the portfolios of the other 20 ministries, including sports, Labor and Social Protection, Health and Education, Science and Technology, the government does not deem 18 million Kenyans, almost one third of the total population, as worthy of a separate ministry. This is a shortcoming we intend to rectify.

Few governments have had youth affairs as a standalone ministry. In the most recent government, youth affairs have been rolled into the Ministry of Public Service, Youth and Gender Affairs. So, in essence, although young women aged 15-34 in this case would be considered 'youth', their affairs are lumped together with those of Gender (one assumes that this includes the 50 percent plus) of women in the country.

Together with Public Service, there is one ministry for 18 million youth, plus 22 million women (subtract the 9 million women who are youth). Having almost 30 million Kenyans' affairs minded primarily by one ministry is a terrible proposition and a lack of appreciation of the importance of youth, now and in the future as they prepare – or at least as we promise that they are getting ready to take the reins of leadership in some future. It is almost as bad as the United Nations taking 65 years to deem women important enough to have more than a few institutes and programs, creating the UN Women.

But even more troublingly, the 2021-2023 (Youth Enterprise Development Fund) YEDF strategic plan hints at what such a strategy involves: the publication's cover features a smiling young woman farmer. Now, there is nothing wrong with a smiling young woman farming (or at least holding a cabbage), but it betrays the reality that we continue to think that youth will carry on with our current economic enterprises, which are overwhelmingly based on agriculture.

The strategic model for the future of the youth is equally dismaying, as though no youth were involved in the formulation of the strategic plan. That said, the board of directors is an impressive array of high-achievers and long-time government employees, potentially a boon if they drive the YEDF into the future, or a huge failure if they are unable to relate to the problems of the youth of Kenya and balance now and future.

There are a number of strategies aimed at the youth, some by individual ministries, such as, predictably, the Ministry of Agriculture, the Ministry of ICT and by the Ministry of Youth Affairs and ~. The YEDP's strategic model leaves something to be desired: it has the funding, but the areas in which it engages youth are rather modest, including access to affordable credit, business development services, developing financial and human capital, mobilizing resources and partnerships, and ICT and infrastructure.[26] We deem these to be insufficient to procure the kinds of changes that the country needs for the majority of its population. There is a need to be more aggressive towards conceiving, planning, articulating and implementing broad and bold visions for our shared future, so that it is one of success.

Other publications begin to hint at the central problems of current planning around youth affairs. For instance, page 3 of the 2019 Youth Development Policy states that, "The Government of Kenya (GOK) and other stakeholders have continued to design and implement various interventions to address the needs of the youth. Some of these interventions include the overarching Kenya Vision 2030 and its associated Medium Term Plans (MTPs); the Sector Plans; the Constitution of Kenya (2010), Devolution and the Big 4 Agenda."[27] It goes on further to outline "The overall objective of the National Youth Policy, Sessional Paper No. 3 of July 2007 [which] was to provide policy framework for addressing issues affecting the youth, notably employment creation, health, education, sports, and recreation, environment, art and culture, partnership and empowerment."[28]

There is a tendency to equate youth with the lowest possible common issue across youth interests – for instance, one thinks of sports, small businesses, farming and other 'domestic' types of support, rather than developing say, libraries, ICT centers or intellectually-based competitions such as designing bikes or motor vehicles. Our national youth strategy, if and where we have one, is woefully inadequate, crafted by older – mostly – men, and is decidedly not forward. It's perhaps sideways-looking, and does not do the youths any favors.

Youth are rarely in decision-making positions in government, and are less frequently invited to the decision-making venues, except as political props. It does increasingly appear that all government does is to 'think for the youth', without a commitment to their peculiar challenges, their overall individual and group welfare, or putting them in the driver's seat of the decisions that the country adopts, and which have effects that will be felt long into the future.

Many public policies speak loftily to the 'inclusion,' of youth, but inclusion by definition implies an outsider who is allowed to be part of a process or situation that they would most usually otherwise *not* be part of. This – the quintessential top-down approach – neither participatory, nor the way to have youth define a future for themselves.

Youth Development Ideas by Actual Youth

There is nothing wrong with being experts at what we are experts at. But if you ever worked in an office with some of the outdated technologies and ideas, and the boss seems to have been around since when the dinosaurs were becoming extinct, you might understand why old men developing 'youth development plans' and strategies, or heading cabinet departments where the most recent technology has to be explained to them is all kinds of problematic.

Honesty demands that we admit that the older we are, the more confounding technology is to us. Research has shown that older people are more skeptical and distrustful of especially more technology, but it is also true that technology is almost doubling in amount and complexity every two years or so. There is also clear evidence that older people are more conservative. If one is in doubt, one just has to look at the past two years when the COVID-19 pandemic has been raging.

There is a risk to tend towards ageism, and one must balance finely between atrophying due to distrust or lack of apprehension of technology, and discriminating against elders.

However, we should admit that youth are more apt at many things, including technology, even as some of our trust in their judgment and decision-making seems to suffer from suspicion. The adage that 'youth is wasted on the young' must not be part of our belief system, and we should embrace the reality that each of us, young or old, has a lot to contribute to this country we all love.

A country that aims to balance the needs of the current generation and leaders (after all, we are railing against the discrimination against elders in the healthcare insurance industry) and the youth, who are 75 percent of the population and the future, can find that balance. But it also ought to acknowledge that youth have been especially marginalized, and that youth input is now vital to move this country towards a future in which they have a stake. After all, they are the most active in issues such as the environment, climate change, conservation, ICT and because they have such a significant stake in the future, one believes that they also have the imperative, and obligation, to create a future in which they will thrive.

The process of deliberating, making and revising government policy must also reflect the place of the youth in the republic. Although the question and format of public input and hearings in the formulation of policy has not been widely implemented and has mostly been perfunctory, it is necessary to reverse this so that we ensure that there is the greatest level of participation in policy-making.

This will also demonstrate the example by which government departments should approach their task of formulating public policy. It will also help bring forth all ideas, in order to arrive at the best policies that will be beneficial to and for all.

Youth Ministry, Youthful Minister

One of our proposals is to create an independent cabinet department, the Youth Ministry, which will be headed by an individual below the age of 34, and preferably a woman. Not only do we signal the commitment to youth empowerment, we are investing in youth to imagine, create and implement their destinies, and further signaling that Kenya is a place of opportunity and membership of and for all – men and women, boys and girls.

Because it would be an almost new creation, the Youth Ministry will absorb the State Department of for Youth Affairs offices and officers, but will also exclusively recruit youth to run the ministry. There might appear to be some risk to this strategy. However, this also gives youth a chance to show that with the proper opportunities, they can be successful and hard-working businesspersons, but also, they have the capacity to drive debates and make sound policy that affects them.

Recognizing that there are two levels of government, and that the National Government cannot alone run affairs for youth, one of the national strategies will be to co-opt County Governments so that they too have youth strategies and potentially, County Executive Committee (CEC) members whose portfolios are not attached to gender, sports and public service.

This is a reasonable strategy, considering that the likelihood that the national youth data is replicated at the County level. We are firmly convinced, based on history, contemporary realities and future possibilities, that empowering, and providing youth with the resources necessary to reimagine the future is a winning strategy not only for them, but for the country as a whole. This is our solemn pledge to our fellow citizens and the nation, if election outcomes should favor this platform.

Youth Strategy for Every Ministry

At the National Government level, besides having the proposed stand-alone cabinet position and portfolio for youth affairs, each cabinet department will be required to come up with a youth strategy. The strategy will require demonstrating that the cabinet department has a strategy that takes into account 70 percent of the population that they serve.

We refuse to allow that the future of the country must be decided solely by this generation, to the exclusion of youth. We also don't believe we abscond on investing and empowering youth while the future belongs to them, especially when we are constantly being reminded, and expressing to the youth, that we are merely borrowing the country from them. Each of the strategies must include input by youth, and to the greatest extent, each cabinet department will see that youth are part of its administrative and strategic decision-making apparatus. This is the path to actually moving from the verbal proposition of giving youth a stake in the future, to actually doing it.

Swap out Program

There is a specific trajectory and time frame for regular government employees to work, gain promotion, perhaps train the new 'replacements' and eventually retire. Government cannot impose retirement upon productive citizens either. However, to the greatest extent possible, the government will offer a swap-out program for voluntary retirees. This program will be akin to a buy-out, where retirees who do so voluntarily will be replaced by youth. Barring the job specifications, when and where possible, the public service will strive to recruit youth under 30.

In the experience of most Kenyans, almost every strike has something to do with job security, pay, benefits, leave, raises or any mix of the spectrum of those issues. The objective of attempting to swap out seasoned employees is to increase the numbers of youth who are entering government service, not only to increase their employment, but to also bring new, fresh ideas to government. The government of the future must look like the future, and the future looks like the youth.

Human Resources and Diaspora Employment Agreements

It is likely that, the worst possible strategy anyone could dream of implementing, especially in dealing with human resources or a population as expansive as the youth, is one that seeks to export youth human resources and abilities by encouraging them to work outside the country and in in the diaspora. But absent a concerted effort to create jobs for the future, it is not clear how the country intends to deal with the 70 percent of the population that is considered youth, especially in light of the fact that Kenya's unemployment is in the region of 40 percent.

Does the government intend to let the 40 percent of the 35.7 million under-35, or 14 million youth, to just waste away, since job creation has clearly not kept up with population growth – or more accurately, population explosion? And we wonder why there is so much drug use and abuse. This is not just about cutting down on drug use; it is also about the loss of revenue that the government faces in future. Government cannot collect taxes on unemployed, except perhaps the VAT that citizens have no choice but to pay or they will starve.

Under these conditions, exporting labor is a viable path to not only provide employment for the 'glut' of fairly well-educated youth, but to also generate remittances. Every study ever has shown that remittances are key contributors to the GDP of many different countries. According to some of the most data and reporting, India received US$87 billion in remittances in 2021, even as COVID-19 raged. If these remittances were sent to Kenya, that would amount to Kshs. 8.7 trillion, which is almost 3 times Kenya's budget.

Elsewhere, about 40 percent of Tajikistan's GDP can be attributed to remittances. The overall value of remittances across the world, at least in the immediate period before COVID-19, was US$540 billion. This far outpaced FDI and ODI figures across the globe, both totaling US$440 billion.[29] Kenya has been a long-time beneficiary of remittances. For example, even with the COVID-19 pandemic ongoing, the Central Bank of Kenya expected remittance flows of US$3.1billion in 2020,[30] a whopping Kshs. 310 billion, and slightly over 10 percent of government expenditure.

It appears then, that rather than continue begging donors and bilateral and multilateral development partners for money, there is an alternative. Pursuing and signing labor agreements abroad so as to deploy Kenyan workers, with a focus especially on countries that have labor shortage and population declines, such as Japan, Italy and other nations in the Arabian Peninsula, would be a most welcome development, and one that we are planning on pursuing vigorously. Remittances are often personal, but facilitate individuals to meet various expenditures: education, health, development projects and even businesses.

There is a further benefit to remittances: for the most part, they are unassailable. Remittances are not susceptible to graft, and if more people are wealthier so that they need the government less, and then government can focus more on citizens living in marginal areas, such as Arid and Semi-Arid

Lands and Regions. We do not underestimate the risk of sending tens, if not hundreds of thousands of Kenyans out to foreign lands, although the alternative of being dependent on government for every little need is also not feasible. We need to invest in youth working, growing and developing socially and economically.

Chapter 10: Research, Development, Tech & Innovation

ଔଔଔ

1. How many patents have been filed and are held by Kenyans (27 in 1998; 294 in 2019 and 2309 between 2010 and 2020[31]), and why are we so intellectually non-productive?
2. Does Kenya invest sufficiently in RDTI and Intellectual Property development? (Kenya Gross domestic Expenditure in Research and Development (GERD) was 0.8% of GDP in 2019)[32] (but higher than 95% Africa and LICs)
3. Do we have a robust ICT policy and what do we do with the creativity Kenyans often exhibit?
4. How can Kenya spur RDTI tailored to her needs and the future, be a leader in Africa and leverage a youthful and educated population to reach these goals better?
5. How are we dealing with personal data and are we securing it against myriad threats arising each day?

Introduction: Research and Development – R & D

Just as precious few countries have developed without industrialization (think the modest-sized Singapore), few have done well without any significant investments in Research and Development, R & D. Research funding can be especially important in spurring a nation to develop new products and services, or to supporting their people, particularly in the academia, to pursue creative activities, obtain patents and develop products that the world needs and is likely to acquire *en masse*. Across the world, there are words, terms and concepts that are synonymous with research, discovery, development and innovation.

Examples abound globally, of brands and manufacturers that we have come to easily recognize. Mention Boeing, and it is clear this is an American company that makes planes, albeit with parts made in many different countries. Consider LG, Samsung, Huawei, General Electric, Volkswagen, Apple and others, and it is clear that these are manufacturing behemoths. In years past, Sony, Mitsubishi, Toyota, Toshiba, Nissan and Fuji evoked Japanese technological prowess. Nothing of manufacture can be said to put Kenya on the map in this manner, unless one considers athletes in this vein.

Technology advances, and so does information, sometimes both simultaneously, sometimes parallel. The products and services connected to them often drive, as much as they are also influenced by the technological advances. Today, some of the most profitable companies (the so-called FAANG, i.e., Facebook (Meta), Amazon, Apple, Netflix and Google (Alphabet)) are tech companies, that technically do not create products, perhaps except Apple, and the others as they move into the field of smart devices. Their genius is in providing services, as MPESA intended. Some of these mix products, services and technology.

Amazon's strategy appears to be predicated upon providing everyone with everything they need, whether it is providing the platforms, storage of goods or space travel. Goods, web services, books, streaming services and even platforms to sell their products are some of Amazon's most profitable ventures. Most technologies that they use are patented and constitute industry secrets. Other technologies such as those of orbiting satellites, Apple's iPhones' schematics, or Facebook's algorithms, are closely guarded industry secrets. It is also alleged that even Coca Cola's century-plus formula, and KFC's recipe, are said to be closely guarded secrets and remain locked away in some vault protected by the 10-headed dragon.

Kenya is in the mix of 'fame' for 'stuff', but for vastly different products and reasons. These are, unsurprisingly, primarily, coffee, tea, long-distance athletics like marathons, and perhaps wildlife. The significance of this, but also the difference – is that none of these are especially derived from R & D.

And frankly, Sri Lanka, Ethiopia, Brazil, Colombia and Algeria can lay claims to at least some of these. Since independence, Kenya has neglected the critical area of R & D, so that the number of patents filed is meager, and the amount of research that is on-going minimal (or probably just poorly explained). As such, we are relegated to the use of already existing technology, knock-offs, sketchy products and near-laughable inventions. Without knocking his invention, the young boy who created an 'automatic hand-washer-sanitizer' at the onset of COVID-19 was widely celebrated, for creating a most rudimentary creation. Even our institutions of higher education have done little to foster a culture of creativity and innovation.

There is a correlation between the educational system, and ability to creatively imagine new products, services or combine products with market conditions so as to create a new service. This is the genius of MPESA. Safaricom did not invent the mobile phone, mobile phone connectivity technology, SIM cards or national IDs. But by combining all of these, it created an exemplary retail banking and telephony system that rivals even those of advanced nations such as the US. The nature of our education system leaves little to the imagination.

The examination administered to assess learning, and the invariability of such testing and systems do not lend themselves to leading to the creation of new products. Home Science might teach students how to make cakes, and Agriculture as a subject teaches – farmers – to grow crops, but no one is trying to invent rockets or new Facebooks. Even Chemistry, where new discoveries (chemicals, elements and new possibilities) might be discovered, the results of the experiments are already known. This is no path to new creations and inventions.

Higher Education Institutions have also failed to break the mold of teaching subjects such as Kiswahili/CRE, which is an excellent combination, but one that does nothing to increase creativity or employability, unless it is to teach the same things or open up a church somewhere. If they are, indeed, creative, they are not necessarily making waves on the international stage to the extent that few patents are filed.

A recent personal discussion with Kenyan high school students on an assessment mode for a class under my tutelage reaffirmed this perspective, on the differences in learning styles that procure different outcomes. In an international relations class taught by this author, students regularly write research papers, which they then present to the class and are critiqued (gently). A second assignment allows students to create podcasts, present their ideas in the form of a video posted to YouTube (with appropriate safeguards e.g., private listing) or write journals and blogs (opinions, anonymously), so that they are actually utilizing applied technology, but also researching and creating new research. And this is at the high school level.

There is a further illustration of the challenges of intellectual property as relates to creative pursuits, whether they occur in research, journals, journal articles and books. Overwhelmingly, Kenyan authors (perhaps besides Ken Walibora and Ngugi wa Thiong'o) do write much more widely, but their books are primarily for the school market. It is probably the only way to make money. A book this author wrote and had published by a leading publisher in 2005 continues to sell, yet the said author has never seen a penny in royalties. Other books published in other countries by the said author have brought in over Kshs. 300,000 in just about three years. Publishing creative works outside of the country robs Kenya access to some of these intellectual opportunities and benefits, including of increasing publications and the taxes that can be collected from the sales.

Purposeful, Directed Changes
Kenya's transformation to a middle (we are absolutely deciding to shun the lower rung) Middle Income Country (this is terribly concerning – why are we not trying to develop even faster) cannot depend on agriculture. In its more than 10,000 years of being practiced, agriculture has never transformed any nation into wealth, at least not on the scale that we need for Kenya to advance, and after all, our economy today is primarily agrarian.

Japan learnt this lesson well in the 1700s. Even though it had one of the most advanced and efficient agriculture-based economies, after a while, there is just not enough land or technology to make agriculture more productive, even as population continued to grow. Besides reaching carrying-capacity, especially Kenya's agricultural inefficiency brooks no future transformation. It is thus most critical that we abandon the 'ostrich strategy' and purpose our changes. Some of these strategies are outlined next, but are by no means the only ones.

RDIT Czar

Previous governments have emplaced an ICT Czar, but this has appeared to be mor of a spur-of-moment appointment than a commitment to ensuring that ICT is a leading part of Kenya's strategy for development and modernization. It is vital that the next government creates a cabinet-level position – and future governments adopt this – a position that is dedicated to research, development, innovation, and technology, not just an ICT Czar. The RDIT Cabinet Secretary and department would have an all-of-the-above strategy, in determining how Kenyan society can integrate technology in most aspects of life, but also in areas of innovation. Thankfully, to a significant degree, various technologies are in use today, the most widespread being in the MPESA phone and payment systems.

The RDIT CS and department will create a strategy for 'all of the above.' Besides coming up with a national RDIT strategy, in a way that overcomes partisan and bureaucratic turf limitations, they will streamline the use of technology so that there are not such obvious gaps in utilization, across all of government and the public sector.

A clear example is to be found in the education field, where almost no widespread use of technology exists, including such software as LMS. While the RDIT CS will have this portfolio, it is necessary that they collaborate with all other cabinet departments and stakeholders in order to infuse research, technology and innovation into each government department beyond any of the currently existing departmental strategies. Their role extends to evaluating current government systems for viability, security and to eliminate the NYS-type scandals.

The next administration will emplace a 'National Competitiveness' strategy separate form that proposes and undertaken through the business-oriented Competition Authority of Kenya (CAK). The goal of this strategy, approach and possibly institution will develop a strategy and series of tasks of a competitive nature with awards financially, as well as providing funding through grants in order to spur competition, especially among the younger people.

The objective of the competitiveness strategy and agency is to spur innovation and apply especially educational and learnt concepts to developing products and services that can be tested for the market. It would also serve as a hub for collaboration and creativity. It is anticipated that this incubator of ideas, concepts and proof-of-concept will also increase our technical capacities.

HEIs and Research Competition

No area is more important in terms of R & D than the research that is conducted in and through higher education institutions. Besides the obvious training role that Higher Education Institutions (HEIs) have, educational institutions are some of the best hubs for research, creativity and innovation. Although Kenya does not have its own 'Silicon Valley', one can see how the concentration of technologies in one region can contribute to concentration of brainpower, so that innovations might ensue.

Together with the 'purposeful' strategies for innovation and creativity, state-funded HEIs will be mandated to create programs that foster innovation, including the development of research and innovation hubs, development of STEM research facilities, seasons and competitions, and teach for the 22nd century, not the 19th. They will also be encouraged, required even, to enter into collaborations with other like-minded institutions around the country, region and the world in order to foster idea exchanges to spur even more research and competition.

There is need to also adjust the approach and strategies in the education sector. Today, some of the best funded areas of study across the world in education are in the so-called Science, Technology, Engineering and Math (STEM), with a dose of arts, which is cited as critical to giving humanity to the technology arena. But in Kenya's HEIs, STEM is neither well-funded, nor driven to new innovations and products. Most of our degree programs are arts-based – nothing wrong with that – but the development of new technologies will not stem from our good recital or acting to imitate Shakespeare, or other arts subjects.

There is a good reason the US recruits and funds STEM graduates from abroad (about 60-80 percent of most STEM graduate students are international students) and then gives them H-1B and Green Cards to enable them to stay, so that they can create and be developers for such companies as FAANG. Although JKUAT was a technology-founded HEI, it cannot be the sole responsibility of one HEI to carry the load for the STEM field. HEIs will be encouraged – and funded – to increase their overall investment in the areas of RDIT.

RDIT – On Innovation, Incubators and Boot Camps
It might sound like a contradiction, that companies and institutions often hold 'hack-a-thons', where some of the best hackers are invited to test the stability of systems before criminals can do the same. Not only does this give the companies themselves some insight into some of what is

possible – what the other side might do to them – but it is also a path to potentially developing new processes and creating new, relevant products.

The RDIT Boot Camps and Incubators will serve a similar purpose, and will supplement the aforementioned competitiveness strategy and institution. The path to innovation manifests through a gathering of the best minds, surrounding them with like-minded citizens, incentivizing them to create new innovations, and finding ways to use those innovations in order to advance business, technology and manufacturing. RDIT Boot Camps ought to even expand, so that as soon as we recover from COVID-19 vagaries and restructure the normal school term, we can begin to put together holiday camps where students learn more than just what's in their school text books.

Ultimately, as a developing nation, we should not, and cannot accept the proposition that Kenyans are relegated to only using things, services and products that others create. This would almost suggest that we accept a lesser station in the greater scheme of things, even though time and time again, Kenyan students who study in western nations almost always do better than their counterparts – so we do know Kenyans are smart. (And some are also fast. Many of them are fast and smart) We know, believe and have to act as though Kenyan students are able to create, just like others around the world, and be part of the conversation about the future of and innovation.

We need to imagine a future in which we are leaders, or at least growing into, where technology, inventions, intellectual property and processes, and opportunity for discovery of 'the next big thing' becomes more than a TV commercial or slogan, but is indeed a national undertaking. Such innovations can and will be sold to the region and to other countries, in a way that rivals some of the better known nations and regions. We will have the vision to not just be an LMIC or MIC; rather, we shall be the leaders of tech innovation and new products.

ICT Infrastructure, Youth, Personal Data and Protection

Kenya has a Ministry of ICT, Innovation and Youth Affairs. We are not even going to address how confusing it must be to have a Ministry of Public Service and Youth Affairs and also have Youth Affairs under the Ministry of ICT with three departments: broadcast and telecommunications, ICT and Innovation and Youth Affairs. One presumes that these are probably connected somehow.

It also appears that the Ministry of ICT has the unenviable job of broadly deciding, and then (de) regulating morally (un)acceptable content (through the Kenya Film Board). Even without attacking the unwieldy nature of the ICT ministry and the seemingly randomly included functions, the structure of these bureaucracies is often as problematic as the work that they do (or that they do not do), and who is at their executive level administrative apparatus.

The 'related organizations' list reads slightly like a group of who atrophied: CA Kenya, KBC, PCK, Year Book, ICT Authority, Media Council, KIMC, NCS and Konza Technopolis Development Authority. Institutions can be important, but none of these especially inspire confidence that we have the best helmed organizations, or that they have adjusted sufficiently to innovate in the services that citizens need. One only has to look at the whole trajectory and even current programming by the government–run KBC, its opportunities and weaknesses, or recall the history of the erstwhile Kenya Posts and Telecommunications

Corporation (KPTC, now split into Telkom and PCK), to see that the leadership and innovation in such organizations lagged behind the pace of development that was needed to move the country into the future of an ICT-savvy nation.

Indeed, the whole adage of 'a picture is worth a thousand words' speaks to this. One of the most interesting marquee pictures on the ICT ministry's website features clearly non-youth persons at some gathering or another. Youth are more likely to (mis)use and benefit more from ICT services than those attendees, but these are the very people in charge of government departments and budgets. And so, this is the place of ICT and youth in this republic; representation is there but not by their kin. Both need to change.

But this is more than about ageism: it is also about how we understand ICT, what we do with it, and how we move forward with it. That older folks are more suspicious of technology (or don't understand it well, or both), is not a secret. Perhaps this is why the country is having so much trouble with managing and implementing legislation.

Government, ICT Policy and Huduma Number

How well is Kenyans' data protected against both hackers and occasional misuse by the government, or even exposure to other citizens who may have no need for that data? Consider for example, the M-PESA withdrawal process. The practices vary (should they?) from place to place, but for the most part, they include a withdrawal, handing over your ID, numbers written in a book that is in plain view of other customers coming in, and then you get your money. In fact, most of us rarely give the whole process another thought or consideration as what might then ensue.

To most people this *process* might seem harmless, but consider how valuable the information that is contained in the ID is, and to what nefarious purposes such information can be put. We won't even propose that Kenya's government systems can be hacked and such information altered, or new documents produced. Actually, we do propose that they can be hacked or otherwise compromised; otherwise, we would not have the NYS type scandals, or the fake land title deeds situations to worry about. Neither will we worry about the potential that if an individual was being stalked by some ill-meaning stalker, that this is a path to their being compromised, event that seems quite likely, even inevitable.

In this context, it seems that Safaricom (and perhaps Airtel and Telkom, but everyone knows the money service sector belongs to Safaricom) and the government are perpetrating dangerous practices. It is also not clear what purpose recording the ID numbers in one place and not in others does. If it is a requirement to record ID numbers, then this should be uniform, but also perhaps, more care should be taken to remove these details and books from public view. If the information is not needed, then the mobile money providers should make this clear and compel the removal and suspension of the books.

As mentioned elsewhere, every Kenyan over 18 has one document in common across the country: the ID. It is used in especially registration of property, which is also a most common shared activity in Kenya. Upon an individual's demise, the ID is one of the most prized possessions for it allows individuals to report the death, and begin to execute the will, or otherwise determine the division of property of the decedent. Considering how counterfeiters have been successful in the past, faking IDs, KCSE certificates and even money, it stands to reason that the probability of personal information being misused is exceedingly, even unacceptably high, and for no good reason whatsoever.

Kenya has a Data Protection Act that dates back to 2019. Its relation to the wider Malabo Convention is not quite apparent (it's not mentioned), but the fact that we are (saying, since we are actually not) protecting data is, ought to be a good thing. However, even with the Data Protection Act, it is especially rich, that these dubious practices continue. Having laws, visions, acts and other legislation is important, but that by itself does not even remotely mean that data is safe. One hopes that the Data Protection Act is supplemented by the strategic vision, although having strategic vision but not doing the bare minimum makes absolutely no sense.

Consider the ICT Ministry's strategic plan. It appears that the way personal information is handled might violate the very government's own Data Protection Act. The handling violates even the most basic tenets of keeping information private. The strategic plan notes the fact that many organizations and companies do indeed collect, store and retain data on Kenyans; "[t]his creates concerns about user privacy, or about the accuracy and the further use of the information by the collecting organisation and any other organisation it decides to share that information with."[33] And so it seems that on the one hand we are concerned, conceptually, about data protection, but practically, this is not the case.

It is evident that any lawyer with a bit of imagination, reading interest and time on their hands might find clauses for which the government and providers could be taken to task for the incongruence that exists, and that is practised, unless we only take data to mean bits and pieces of 0s and 1s. For instance: in the 2019 Data Protection Act, Part IV—Principles and Obligations of Personal Data Protection, Article 43 (1) reads thus: "[w]here personal data has been accessed or acquired by an unauthorised person, and there is a real risk of harm to the data subject whose personal data has been subjected to the unauthorised access..."[34]

The Act then proceeds to outline how reporting of data exposure and perhaps even violations should be done. It appears that the Office of the Data Commissioner should be inundated with all manner of complaints, because every time anyone hands over their ID and their details are entered into that ignominious book, it appears to be a violation of the Data Protection Act. But in this context, Kenya's gap between the law and its application continues to show a deficit, not in just this issue, but across a host of other issues.

The Law – or (In)Justice] Steps In

Kenyans are identified by a number of 'number categories' that are assigned to them throughout their lives. None of these numbers often relate to any of the others, and for the most part, these can be many, and confusing. If the goal was to confuse any potential data hackers and misuse, this would make sense, although they started before there were any concerns for data protection in the age of information.

To illustrate the profound proliferation of numbers, most Kenyans will have a birth certificate number (interestingly, that is not the number on the document, it is the oddly-named 'entry number,' possibly an admission number (3, to the 3 levels of schools), an ID number (which also has a serial number), a Passport Number (with an immigration record number), a voter register card and number, driver's license number and other random numbers such as KCSE registration, NHIF, etc. Enter Huduma Number and NEMIS.

If the objective of the Huduma Number was to consolidate all these numbers into one identity, it would make lots of sense, and be warranted. By the way, why aren't the ID numbers consolidated? The thinking behind the Huduma Number and card would be sound if it was intended to function like a Social Security Number (SSN) that is used in the US and that is one of the most fundamental IDs. On the other hand, we have a tendency to hybridize insufficiently, so that it our product is almost the worst of all outcomes.

But the haphazard implementation, without any public participation as required by Kenya's constitution or sensitization of the public as to what the number does and why it is important or different from the ID number almost spelt a death knell to the number. But in our estimation, this is not the greatest weakness to the Huduma Number. The greatest weakness is that it would appear that the implementation of the number violated the government's own rules, i.e., the Data Protection Act of 2019.

This point was driven home by the 14th October, 2021 High Court ruling in Kenya. The ruling struck down the government's decision to issue the Huduma Number cards. The reasoning was that the government had "started collecting personal data from Kenyans without first determining how it would protect that data." Further, it was found that it had "not appreciated the import and the extent of the application of the Data Protection Act with respect to the collection and processing of data under the National Integrated Identity Management System [NIIMS]."[35] This is a stinging rebuke and repudiation of government's actions, but more importantly, that the government, the *Leviathan*, is violating its own policy speaks to the haphazard way we think of the information on 55 million Kenyans.

Even if the government were to appeal and potentially win on an appeal, it really does have to learn that a patched up broken egg is still a broken egg. No one seems to have an idea, and government has not provided a good explanation, on why the Huduma number is needed, what it will do, what it will not do, and perhaps why citizens need it, given that the citizen has a birth certificate, ID card, passport, voter's card, bank cards, KCPE and KCSE Index numbers, all which are different. But the lofty goals of data protection that might involve banking, medical, and property information and so on are important, but there are basic things that the government could do, and which affect more Kenyans.

The government itself needs to up its game, and cease being one of the biggest violators of its own Data Protection Act. The government is a regulator of business and industry, and ought to be looking at data protection loopholes by both public and private entities. For example, the idea that those M-PESA books (Airtel and Telkom withdrawals are less clear), are out in the open is a clear DPA violation. Placing students' academic results and their performance on exams, on notice boards that are in the open with free public access is also an issue; it violates – minors' – educational rights without parental input or consent.

There are other areas of great concern relating to the amount, visibility, storage and use of data. Visitors' signups in places such as the National Museums of Kenya (NMK) or the Kenya National Archives, where individuals' name, ID number and phone number are on a counter book are perhaps the most egregious violations by government institutions. One wonders what would happen if someone took a picture of these and posted it online, and what kinds of nefarious activities might result. It is not even clear that these sign-ins serve any useful purpose.

It is time to treat data and personal information as protected, valuable, personal and in need of greater protection than we currently require or practice. Considering that we do the same with hospital records and medical information (one assumes they might include patient ID), we need to stop exposing them and decide to actually implement data protections in the best traditions of such practices.

Although we are not quite suggesting that Kenya adopt the EU-style General Data Protection Regulation 2016/679 (commonly known as GPDR), it seems that personal information should be better protected. There should be further, and urgent deliberation, of the incongruence between the idea of data protection, and the ways in which we expose a lot of citizens' data. Educational records and performance that is posted on notice-boards is data. So is the data that is often generated when one does an MPESA withdrawal and the attendants write down the person's ID number and whatever else they put down, on an exposed page of their book. So is data shared, when one signs in to visit the Museum or the National Archives. Data cannot just be electronic.

Chapter 11: Public Service and Human (In)security

☙❧☙❧☙❧

1. Why are public security agent, apparatus and overall, policy, unable to contain often sporadic but regularly persistent conflict especially in areas of the Rift Valley?
2. Between training and tradition, what informs the police's poor attitude towards the public and treatment as though they were criminals? (consider arrest mechanisms)
3. How can we incentivize public (security) service so as to eradicate corruption that leads to insecurity in Kenya?
4. What strategies can be implemented to ensure long-term human security for Kenyan citizens and residents and who / what are the most significant inputs required?

Introduction

Whereas there exists a parallel universe in which Kenya and other African countries are seen as very dangerous places to visit, be present and live in, one can only assume that it is because of the wildlife. However, nothing is nearly as important as security across its entire spectrum, perhaps except Maslow's basic needs, which incidentally include elements of security. Providing security is one of the most critical functions of a government.

Historically, and going back to Hobbes, the proposition of an all-powerful Leviathan who will (as later argued) exercise monopoly over all violence, was central to the formation of government. The broad reasons for formation of government have remained largely the same. Today, around the world and just as often in Kenya, insecurity is the leading cause of displacement, hunger, weapons proliferation, underdevelopment and all manner of other sub-optimal outcomes.

Providence has mostly been kind to Kenya, for there has never been the Rwanda-level type of violence and insecurity, even though we always seem to be flirting with the possibility particularly around elections. However, we have still seen and even experienced issues of insecurity, and for a while, we were leaning in the direction of the most significant conflicts in the region. One of the most critical issues that contribute to state failure is insecurity, and its larger cousin, conflict.

There is no nobler goal than to continue to assure security, peace and harmony for a country's citizens. Yet even as we aspire towards this goal, it is evident that parts of the country do not share this implied tranquility. How can government make sure that security is maintained, and that whenever insecurity arises, it is quickly contained?

One might presume that security is related to the level of armed that a society shows. However, even a cursory review of news reports suggests that in areas where Kenyan citizens possess more guns, levels of insecurity are higher, as are banditry, killings and interpersonal violence. Being armed can often deter some criminal activity but is no guarantee of security. But considering other countries, Kenya's guns held outside of the military forces are far fewer than in other countries, which have more guns but also more homicides and crime.

A most important example of this is the United States. It has 393 million guns, or close to 46 percent of the global total of all individual (non-military), privately held firearms. This computes to 120.5 firearms for every 100 individuals.[36] There are literally more people than guns in the US, and not by a small margin – in fact, the number of civilian guns exceeding the US population is larger than Kenya's population. It is a wonder then that only about 16,000 persons are victims of intentional homicides each year, although if one adds the suicides and accidental discharges of guns, suicides, etc., the figure approaches 50,000.

Guns are not the answer: they have never been, and as the US has shown, the proclivity to use weapons even for the smallest disagreements increases the risk to individuals and to society as a whole, whether from the accidents or criminality. But there is a variety of ways in which the country can assure that every citizen feels safe and secure. Initiatives such as the 'Nyumba Kumi' are important, but we must also remember that majority of Kenyans, almost 60 percent, live in rural areas, and so the concept may not be as practical here. Providentially, rural Kenyans tend to be much more familiar with each other and even know of the 'suspicious characters' among them.

Thus, criminal activity is, on average fairly low, although during elections, we seem to lose some of that neighborliness and frequently fight each other. Low levels of crime is a positive element of Kenyan society and should be celebrated. Still, there are other types of crime that occur: of passion, or petty variety e.g., stealing of goats and sheep and chicken. It is necessary for the government, at both county and national levels, to continue to fulfill their roles to secure their citizens.

Public Service: Focus on Security

Electricity, water and sewer services are important to provide to the citizenry. However, these pale in comparison with the provision of security as a public service. In fact, few governments, perhaps excepting local government, exist to provide the former. We institute government to improve collective welfare and security, not dispose of waste better. Although individuals are remunerated (one hopes well, but fears not), for their services especially as public security officials, be they police officers or chiefs and related functions, their work qualifies as a 'public trust' office. These are not positions that are simply 'doing the work.'

Where such positions exist even outside Kenya, it is argued that "public trust positions are positions that perform work that involve a significant degree of public trust and confidence that the [...] official will carry out the work in accordance with applicable laws, regulations and guidelines."[37] Nothing could be worse than abusing public trust, particularly when one aims to enrich themselves by essentially robbing the public, who have entrusted the management of such positions to them. The lack of a recourse – considering that public trust positions are also positions of power – make the issue even more important.

There exists little benefit in pointing fingers at who has done what, when, and moving forward in positions of public trust might require those compromises that we are loath to make – have people admit to their abuses, maybe fine them, and then move on to build a better republic – after all, pointing fingers to those who own and are ready to use guns sounds self-defeating, but it is necessary to deal with the lack of trust in, and ethics of individuals appointed to public trust positions.

It is self-evident that even within Kenya's public service, particularly in those areas that are critical to human well-being, including security, public service needs individuals who are committed to discharging their obligations with the best traditions of satisfaction arising from the service itself and the service they render, rather than from fleecing innocent Kenyans. The security domain is especially important, and hypothetical situations can often shed light on what we often trifle with when public service in the security sector is compromised.

Kenya has experienced a number of major terrorist attacks, including against the US Embassy in 1998 (200+ deaths), the Westgate Shopping Mall shooting starting September 21, 2013 (71 deaths) and the Garissa University College attack on 2nd April 2015 (with 148 deaths). Though we have not been privy to the postmortems of what went wrong with public security apparatus so that such a heinous attack was possible, one can't help but wonder if there were security lapses that were occasioned by public officers 'looking the other way.'

Often, the past is the predictor of the future. We have all (or mostly) seen that note pass hands at the police roadblock, with nary a glance at who is riding where and what they may be carrying. Did security perhaps let through a truck that was full of explosives or carrying boxes of ammunition for automatic weapons used in the attack? Did they look the other way and take the prescribed Kshs. 50 even as a bus (or private vehicle) ferrying automatic weapons and tens of thousands of lethal rounds passed through the many police checkpoints? We may as well never know, unless someone someday 'fesses up. We might always wonder about those checkpoints.

Speaking of checkpoints, past events are often predictors of future events. It is on the very rare occasion that a vehicle is ever detained at the mandatory police checkpoints, for being unroadworthy or even potentially carrying contraband – although the latter would be difficult to detect, with just one's nose as the extent of the equipment provided to the officers. But how many of us have driven behind a vehicle that was emitting such noxious smoke that we were not sure we would survive without being choked to death? One reckons quite a number.

Perhaps we are just lucky that Kenya is such a low-stakes country for terror or other nefarious, violent non-state actors to attack, because it is wide open for anyone who might have ill-intent. A recent trip taken from Arusha to Nairobi will likely illustrate this point. From forged travel passes to foreign nationals getting off vehicles and rejoining them past the checkpoints or simply 'incentivizing' their crossing, our security leaves a lot to be desired, and rarely inspires confidence besides providence's grace. One hopes that there was a good reason to not obtain the proper travel documents, but again, have we not seen the cases of nefarious actors going into countries using these loopholes?

Armed (in) security

Public servants who work in the security sector are invaluable to the security and well-being of the Kenyan citizen and polity. Police Officers, prison warders, paramilitary services and the military are essential to the overall security architecture of this country, even, but particularly when the country faces such attacks as the Westgate Mall or at the Garissa University and are asked to respond to frequently life-and-death situations.

They run into danger, or guard sometimes violent offenders who including murder suspects and convicts. Except perhaps in Costa Rica, where the military does not exist, the military is important in not only national security and in the occasional call to fight for the nation; they also perform other services to include emergency rescue operations.

Police officers are perhaps the closes and most 'interacted with' group of law enforcement. There are both good and sometimes less than perfect instances of interactions between the police and the public. Yet we must acknowledge that both carrying a weapon and confronting criminals are high-stakes asks, but also, that to equip such officers with the right gear and skills is also part of what we as a country should do.

As much as we occasionally denigrate police officers for petty (and sometimes major) corruption, it must be considered that the system both provides incentives, and imposes no costs, except the occasional camera-in-the-bushes that captures one or two incidences, compared to the tens of thousands of matatu trips that end up with a Kshs. 50 note tucked under the driver's door and surreptitiously collected. Poor pay, conditions of service and a leadership culture that condones corruption is partly to blame. The fact that police officers can make up stuff and turn it into law that regular citizens violate also contributes to the rational choice outcome of choosing graft.

If a police officer, for example, seeking 'unga', alleges that some citizen smells like 'bhang', they do not need to prove that the 'suspect' smoked. If the matter can be 'settled' at, say, Kshs. 100, then everyone benefits. As Kenyans, we have to find alternatives to these types of street justice and their implications for graft, whether it is from being armed with cameras on their persons, to ensure that any allegations are either supported by evidence, or are dismissed and such conduct eliminated from among the forces. It is not our destiny to be among the most corrupt nations on the planet.

On the issue of security, there have been conversations in the public arena, over whether or not private security guards should be trained and armed with guns and other types of firearms. This is an important debate, considering that arming security guards at a major factory with batons counts for really weak security. One wonders how such guards could ever hope to stop armed robbers, and gives the impression that the guards are mere props. Conversely, we acknowledge that security guards are not as similarly trained, paid or supervised as the police or the military.

We consider it reckless, to even consider arming the security guards who at present, are poorly trained as private guards – and in some instances, not even trained. However, perhaps allowing less lethal forms of protection, while on duty, can be considered and proposed, but even then, with some standardized training. These non–lethal forms might include, for instance, tasers. While they are fairly lethal and may stop any potential criminal intending the business harm, they are unlikely to be as misused and be as frightful as guns might be.

But on that note, it is perhaps important, and timely to consider police remuneration – but more importantly, that of prison warders. A dated visit to the Athi River GK Prison a few years ago left me in great consternation, and worried about both the security of the inmates and of the officers. The officers' housing was essentially adobe, thatched huts, with open sewers and toilets no human should have to use – communal at that.

One hopes that the living conditions of the prison guards / warders have improved since then, because there cannot possibly be anything more dangerous than paying any person – not just these prison guards (or more precisely, the level of Constables) Kshs. 21,000 a month *and equipping them with an automatic sub-machine gun.* As much as we want to believe in the better angels of our nature, to quote Lincoln off-subject, that is a lot of power for people we pay Kshs. 21,000 a month. This is far much lower pay than even a driver or a tout, who ordinarily do not carry guns – and I am unsure we would give them guns.

We assign the prison officers an awesome responsibility but fail to pay them even a living wage. We often do the same for the individuals we assign the protection of our elites – when they function as chase drivers for governors and other elected officials. One suspects that there is a . Kshs. 21,000 is a mere US$6.1 per day, which is only about 3x above the UN-defined poverty level. But, we must also acknowledge that this is only the equivalent of US$800 above the US$1,400 per capita GDP. It is not clear that this is sufficient for individuals with such responsibility.

Banditry and Illegal Arms

Kenya has significant lengths of, and at that, immensely porous borders, through which all manner of goods and especially illegal contraband comes through on a near-daily basis. One hopes that most of the contraband that comes into the country is clothes and other stuff for which merchants do not want to pay taxes, but one fears that this may not be quite accurate. Is it possible that it is also a conduit for illegal firearms entering the country? Guns, illegally owned and held especially in parts of North and North-western Kenya, are a constant menace, and nothing has seemed to work to rid the region of the guns. Not even gun buy-backs seem to put paid to the proliferation and use, especially in the perennial banditry and cattle rustling. activities

Making matters even worse, Kenya is surrounded by countries that share ethnically homogeneous populations. The populations have been historically shared populations and even after current borders were imagined, they remained across the borders. It would be a significant challenge to police these borders or close them; it is actually the lesser evil to leave them open. Kenya's neighbors also have a history of conflict, and proliferation of small arms: Somalia, South Sudan and eastern Uganda. How can these guns be contained?

It is not clear that there is a magic bullet that will allow for the gun menace to disappear. But it appears that applying an 'all-of-the-above' strategy might begin to at least reduce the menace that is experienced by such populations. While we do not advocate arming teachers or anything of that scale, it is useful for the government (both national and county) to interface with the community leaders, for peace cannot be found without conversations: you cannot shake hands with a closed fist.

Engaging even with those suspected of cattle rustling and some of the banditry, to the extent that they have not committed especially egregious crimes, is necessary. We should broker peace, establish patrol zones, and identify individuals who may be less likely to be rustlers or bandits and ensure that they are part of the security apparatus, even if they don't need to fight.

Conflict is one of man's historical, and now perennial challenges, but on the other hand, these are indeed intractable problems. They will take time and effort, and it is not clear that the solution is currently known; otherwise, one trusts the government would have implemented it. Still, it is a commitment to find a solution to these issues. Some of these might require the disarmament of persons who believe that their security can only lie at the end of a gun barrel. We need to solve this.

Police Extrajudicial Killings

Whereas the past few years seem to have witnessed a decrease in the number of individuals who have met their unfortunate end at the suspected hands of the police, there is some record of extra-judicial killings. In fact, the June-July months of 2021 saw spirited protest over the disappearance and killing of two brothers just after the hand started their business, allegedly at the hands of police on suspicion of violating curfew.

In the early days of the curfew during the COVID-19 period, more Kenyans were killed (and publicly whipped by police) than were killed by COVID-19. There is no good reason why an individual should be a) whipped b) sat down two hours before curfew and detained, possibly to be financially exploited. It is such rogue officers that ought to be prosecuted to the fullest extent of the law *and* made examples of.

These and other killings and whippings have smacked of callous disregard for life, and of a force that contains rogue elements, or poor leadership, or both. We would hate to think that police and paramilitary leadership condones the clear and obvious violation of Kenyans' human rights and the right to assemble peacefully, or that they abrogate themselves the immunities to suggest that the callousness runs so deep that nothing happens to their rank and file when they do.

While we concede that police do a good job of maintaining law and order, but the license to maintain law and order is not a license to kill anyone. Any instance of police extra-judicial killings ought to be condemned and prosecuted, although this speaks to perhaps a more significant issue, of the relationships between law enforcement law and citizens they serve.

Another disturbing reality pervades: the idea that there are killings whose perpetrators are never found is both disheartening and frightening to the ordinary citizen, but when government agents are accused of extracting the ultimate price on one of the citizens without the benefit of prosecution, this is quite troublesome. A next IG of police will have a most noble task of ensuring that the dark days of police extrajudicial killings have been truly left in the past.

Arresting Citizens: Methods

Police officers are not juries or executioners. There is a reason why courts exist. The job of the police officer is to arrest suspected offenders and prosecute them based on the so-called 'books.' The wanton whipping of Kenyan citizens for whatever reason is especially unwarranted; it is also a violation of individuals' human rights that ought to, and should have been prosecuted to the fullest extent of the law.

While whipping and use of horses may be a tactic for crowd control (there are other tactics for crowd control that do not involve whipping, including the use of tear gas, the terrifying horses and tear gas), the risk of injury is especially grave. Police and paramilitary officers should recall that Kenyans have a right to assemble and to protest without infraction of these rights through whipping. And they should not be dispersed for exercising a constitutional right, however much the authorities might dislike such displays. Even school children are no longer whipped these days – we are clearly past that.

Kenyan law is based on presumption of innocence, until one is proven guilty or not. We are not the French, who allegedly presume guilt and require proof of innocence. That said, arrests in Kenya leave no doubt that the police are convinced that the suspect is guilty even before they make it to court. To pull a suspect by their belt in the small of their back, and then marching them "kama mwizi" on tiptoes is unnecessary, humiliating and serves no lawful or constraining purpose.

It is incumbent upon police leadership to properly train, or retrain police officers in the art of arresting or detaining citizens. It is time to treat even accused Kenyans as individuals who retain their dignity and rights even while under arrest. Yes, some may protest arrest, but in a country where gun ownership is scarce and therefore any possible risk of harm to officers diminished, it is important avoid humiliations to citizens. And there is no better description of whatever the police do to detain a citizen than simply, humiliation.

Instead, the arresting officer(s) should calmly inform a citizen that he is under arrest and to explain the crimes or infractions they are suspected of committing. There are outstanding processes all around the world, that we could borrow, adopt and even improve, as we detain citizens. One thinks, off the bat, of the US' *Miranda Warning*. And we should also ensure that even the accused can access representation. There are far too many individuals arrested and accused and coerced into a confession here or there, especially out of fear.

It is our goal to restructure how individuals are placed under restraint or arrest, with the process being dignified. After all, aren't they innocent until proven guilty? Once they are arrested, arraignment should be expedited, on account of our police cells being less than the most hospitable places to hold anyone. Our laws have progressed to require that suspects be produced in court sooner, but especially in non-violent crimes, bonding out of jail and awaiting a court date should be encouraged, to reduce overcrowding and the spread of diseases, bugs and all manner of misery in remand facilities.

Detention with Dignity

Incarceration is part of how society deals with offenders, and as such, we expect that it is part of our society. Many reports on the conditions of most prisons are almost always disheartening, notwithstanding the sometimes smiling women (and men) on visits by important officials. One is unsure if there is less *ugali* if they don't smile on cue.

It is not clear that the current incarceration facilities and policies are meant to rehabilitate convicted offenders. Kenya's facilities are also not necessarily sufficiently separated so that petty offenders are in low-security facilities. To have murderers serving jail sentences alongside petty offenders, e.g., individuals convicted of petty theft, is absolutely unhelpful. Or maybe it is helpful, for it trains those petty offenders to become better criminals *a la* John Kiriamiti of the fictional *My Life in Crime* fame. We must commit to rehabilitation, but to also building minimum security prisons where those who have been incarcerated might be more easily reintegrated into society.

We should also aim to borrow best practices from among other societies. While some crimes may call for incarceration, advanced nations have perfected the spectrum of how to aid convicts go through their sentences. For instance, an individual who is working and happens to be convicted of a felony like DUI or DWI often serve their jail sentence on weekends, reporting to the jail on Friday evening, leaving Sunday evening.

That an individual gives up freedom but continues to thrive in society (for example if they have a full time job), allowing them weekend incarceration is important because the individual pays for their crime, but also keeps working and thus does not depend on the government for sustenance, as they would if they lost their job or were incarcerated full time. Some might argue that this risks people running away, considering how challenging it is to find people in Kenya, but if one has a job, one imagines that they would like to keep it and would do their time quietly to avoid more complications.

Human Security: Freedom from Fear

There is a different version of security, which is equally important. This is the notion of human security. It is not enough to live in a fear—free environment: it is also critical that individuals live in communities that are safe and secure, where they are unafraid of such occurrences as being stripped because of the choice of clothes they wear, how they look, or who they love. This is a more substantive, national conversation. But it is vital to ensure that security of individuals is enforced, assured.

That women are disrespected, cat-called, or otherwise sexually harassed is not new, or surprising. What is surprising is our reactions, and the idea that we have almost accepted it. We dismiss this as 'it's just what guys do.' This cannot be 'business as usual.' It is good philosophy, to consider (with limits) if each woman was one's sister, daughter, or mother, and how hard we would fight for these 'our women.' We should be willing to fight for *all* women and to treat them the way we want 'our women' treated. It is definite that most men would fight to the death for their mothers and perhaps daughters.

It is not clear how to go about making such changes so that each woman and girl feels respected, treasured, cherished and is able live security with and in human security and dignity. These are not issues we can legislate, require or enforce. Respect is human, societal, but we must endeavor to accord all Kenyan citizens (and foreign residents), especially women and girls, the respect and dignity that each individual hopes for and deserves; the same respect that we would accord our most cherished. It strikes one that if their mother was cat-called, there might be a vigorous fight. This is the respect that should be accorded all women and girls; this is not always the case.

Domestic Violence: A Plague upon Us

The issue of domestic violence has been addressed elsewhere, but it is important to consider this issue from a public service of the security flavor perspective. While we might want to dismiss domestic violence as part of the issues that should be dealt with in the domain of the homestead, there are most nefarious outcomes of domestic violence.

For instance, on December 20th, it was reported that a man burnt his wife to death after chopping off her fingers following a domestic violence incident, in which the husband alleged that the wife had acquired a mobile phone from a love interest, which she was using to communicate with the love interest. This is not only traumatic, but the essence of murder, from what might be considered to be domestic violence. While it is not clear that the matter had been previously reported to the police, in the same region, a man also killed his wife and 3 kids in yet another domestic violence (a.k.a. violent murder) event.

It is necessary to stem the clearly rising tide of intimate partner, domestic and gender-based violence, murder, maiming and other mayhem that is causing untold trauma to families and even the nation, neighbors who have to hear the screams of a woman who then is killed in a fire. And this is not isolated by any measure. The number of cases are rising, and it is incumbent to find solutions so that we are not losing women, girls and whole families needlessly and painfully. There are always good (and often bad) ideas all around us, some we can borrow and implement.

In certain jurisdictions in the US, any report of a domestic violence or disturbance requires that one of the parties (especially the aggressor, i.e., the one who likely did not report the incident) to leave the home, because a) there are more guns than people and b) people do tend to 'resolve' domestic incidences in terrible ways. In fact, statistics show that 52 percent of all homicides are committed by an intimate partner. We must change how we deal with domestic violence incidences, and commit to creating allyship so that we can reduce the instances of domestic violence and save the lives of especially women in these potentially life-threatening situations.

While such a solution may be misplaced in a blueprint for *A Better Kenya*, it is critical to use the current, existing strategies and mechanisms to deal with GBV and IPV. From counseling to therapy to providing safe havens, such as shelters for survivors of domestic and intimate partner violence, there should be a concerted effort by both government and by private, non-governmental organizations, to not only support survivors, but to deal with the causes and provide tools to assist couples to survive the conditions that they find themselves in. Many spouses stay within these abusive relationships due to the lack of alternatives. We aim to ensure that this is no longer the case, and that alternatives and some support exists to ensure that we are not burying women and children who become victims of some of these domestic violence situations.

Uniformed Services and Standards for Evidence

Increase pay, benefits and conditions of service, and to some extent, the levels of supervision. Today, technology exists, that can vastly improve policing. The past has shown us that sometimes, process is not followed in making arrests, and this has led to unfortunate outcomes. While there are an estimated total of 100,000 police and paramilitary officers, we can require that the service become even better *and* accountable.

We should equip police officers with more cars and other means of transport. In the same vein, police cars ought and should be equipped with video cameras, and police officers be outfitted with body cameras. In order to root out graft, and considering the history of coerced (or strongly encouraged) confessions, we would require that prosecutions be supported by not only police reports, but also video evidence.

There is no clear purpose to police roadblocks, other than the nefarious purposes of 'collecting road tax.' Where these roadblocks are erected, it would be necessary to place equipment that might ensure that monitor the proceedings, both for the security and safety of the officers, but also, to ensure that any violations are documented and supported by credible evidence. As we have seen elsewhere, even public servants such as the police are human and therefore fallible.

Further, in the age of the internet, M-PESA and other methods of monitoring, it is important to ensure that – and this should apply to both elected officials and anyone in public service as a condition of continued employment – individuals are not living beyond their means.

At the same time, improving the overall working and service conditions for public officers especially in the security arena is especially critical and long overdue. These include pay, housing, medical and retirement, among others. We should make it so valuable to be in the uniformed services that those who enter will serve with dedication and excellence, and will have every intention of avoiding separation on account of such iniquities as petty (or major) graft. After all, isn't this seen in police forces in other countries? Why are we different?

They say it is near impossible to teach old dogs new tricks. However, as optimists, we anticipate that some, if not most, of these changes, including others that might be proposed by the members themselves and vetted by the relevant hiring authority, will produce a happier workforce, rid individuals of the need and guilt of having to supplement income and/or collect 'taxes' on behalf of the numerous nameless 'higher-ups,' and instill more confidence in public service in the security sector.

Chapter 12: Regionalism, Global Diplomacy and Defense

ഗ౿ഗ౿ഗ౿

1. What is Kenya's history and role in regional conflicts and diplomacy, and are we good neighbors?
2. How can we be more effective in securing our own internal peace and supporting regional peace efforts?
3. What are some of the most egregious things we have done against our neighbors and the region and why?
4. Going forward, what is Kenya's role in the EAC and IGAD, AU and the international community?

Introduction: Our Foreign Policy Preferences

Kenya's foreign policy is often a mix of intrigue and clarity in some of the choices by leaders, but it is rarely articulated or even explained. One surmises that if a poll were conducted on Kenyans on what our foreign policy is, it is quite likely that blank stares would issue. For although we seem to cooperate with other countries in the region, the issue of foreign policy making is as ambiguous to citizens, with nary a clue as to what is important to the republic, and is seen as 'government work.'

Perhaps this is warranted: foreign policy rarely touches most ordinary citizens' lives, for theirs are mostly lives within certain radii and going to Nairobi is a trip. Those with passports to travel to other countries do not regularly seem to need help, or know that they can most likely find help at the end of their arm, apart from during the COVID-19 crisis and the subsequent repatriation of citizens from China, where they had been stuck and allegedly, variously mistreated and kept in subhuman conditions.

That said, the lack of widespread appreciation of what our foreign policy is, is no reason to *not* have a robust foreign policy and to articulate it to citizens, unless we don't believe they have an interest, or a say, in how we relate with others in the region and afar. Most suggest that foreign policy is mostly the domain of major powers, but even we smaller powers have our own preferences, interests, dilemmas and opportunities for both cooperation and conflict. Quite often, we see and–or hear our leaders speaking about Kenya's commitment to positive relations with Africa and the world, and this is to be cheered.

Some elements of working with the world includes cooperating with other nations, especially those in this region, and supporting common human endeavors such as the environment, human rights, hosting the many who find themselves displaced and who seek refuge within her territory, the eventual refugee resettlement, being an advocate for the peaceful settlement of disputes and finding peace in the region. This is part of the DNA of the Kenyan foreign policy doctrine (which rather interestingly, remains unarticulated). Kenya's standing in the international arena is decent and there is much to celebrate for all that the nation has achieved in its young existence.

Past presidents have even branched out and set out on a different foreign policy and diplomacy course. President Kibaki in particular started the so-called pivot to the East, which our Kenyan-American President later almost repurposed (he spoke of the Pacific). It does appear that the pivot has paid dividends, with China becoming an important development partner. The building of roads, railways and the ports is one of the most tangible outcomes of the shift in foreign policy.

It is important and necessary to make friends and turn any potential enemies into friends. After all, this is vital to ensure that there are no threats to the homeland and allows for greater spending on other issues of importance to Kenya. There are, of course, occasional tiffs, none so pressing as to not be solvable through the efforts of diplomacy and institutions in the region and around Africa. One recalls the 2008 crisis and is gratified that countries in the region, the broader world and especially the African Union recognized the value of Kenya as an oasis on a continent with a bit of conflict.

Cooperation with regional neighbors and AU missions is vital. But more important is the role that Kenya has played in the region, being a bastion for peace, hosting international offices, diplomats and concerns. It is quite evident that Kenya's place as a haven where groups and persons fleeing conflict have found refuge speaks to our place in regional and global affairs.

It also perhaps explains the support that Kenya garnered as it vied for a third stint at the UN Security Council (UNSC). Granted, this was a hard-fought battle against Djibouti, which is a member of IGAD, but the idea that Kenya was the official AU candidate speaks to some of the things we have done right. The eventual result left no doubt that we still command the respect of the continent and world, particularly given that many African countries have never served on the UNSC. That said, Kenya does still face some challenges.

Kenya's Foreign Wars

Kenya has fought two major wars in its almost 6 decades of existence, both against Somalia. It also threatened to respond and deployed soldiers in 1976, to the Ugandan border, but that was predictable and necessary considering who Amin was. Jomo Kenyatta was president when the first (*Shifta*) war commenced. His son inherited the second war which began in 2011.

One cannot decisively say that the wars were conclusively decided, or necessarily justify especially the second one. The wars did put a bit of a dent in the narrative that Kenya was a peace-loving nation, although our claim is that Somalia or its agents was the aggressor in essentially both cases. An irredentist Somalia regularly invites all manner of intervention, including by Ethiopia. While its status as a failed state makes any attempt at new irredentism mostly patchwork, and more likely to break up into clan enclaves than to unite as a unified Somali state, there was probably a need to put that particular genie back in the bottle, and discourage other such future aspirations.

The history, conflict and overall narrative of the Kenya vs. Somalia issue is much more complex, including the perception that Kenyan Somalis have long expressed. This is the perception that both the British colonial government and its successor, the new Kenyan government, were neglecting them and that in the first place, they were not part of Kenya – and there is some historical support for that view. Today, Kenyan Somalis speak of 'going to Kenya', partly explaining he sentiment over support for secession. No nation likes to split up, and in this case, Kenya was fortunate that it wasn't split up. Indeed, Sudan and Ethiopia give some validity to this perspective.

The second time that Kenya took up arms against Somalia – some suggest that more precisely, Kenya was the aggressor and invaded Somalia – was much more confounding. This was in part because the intervention occurred fully 20 years after Somalia first collapsed as a juridical state. In fact, before the 2011 invasion, World Islamic Courts had come and gone, and until then, Kenya had not found an urgent reason to fight Somalia. True, a few western tourists had gone into Somalia and been kidnapped, but any western tourist who goes into Somalia may have other significant issues. Like maybe a misapprehension of that terrorism and perceived western imperialism is.

It is hard to argue that Kenya's ill-advised sojourn into Somalia was not responsible for, or at least the trigger for the Westgate Shopping Mall and Garissa University attacks which killed scores of Kenyans who likely had no opinion on Kenya's need to be fighting in Somalia. It is also extremely hard to see how Kenya benefited from this jaunt into Somalia. No one can credibly say that, as a result of the excursion, Kenya subsequently became safer. In fact, the opposite is true. Besides these high-casualty events that rocked the country, the El Adde debacle that we pretended didn't happen is another yardstick of how flawed the thinking and actions of invading Somalia were.

As a country, it is important to recognize that not every situation can be fixed with the force of arms, and most certainly, not for a country as weakly protected as Kenya often appears to be. Most military interventions end badly for the intervening power (just ask the US in almost everywhere – Iraq, Afghanistan, Vietnam...or the former Soviets with Afghanistan). It must be our objective to avoid military intervention at all cost and in all instances except when directly attacked or invaded. Diplomacy works and nothing good has ever come from any of our military interventions in Somalia the   two   times   we   intervened.

Global Player: UN Presence

Kenya is one of the few African nations that have the unique distinction of hosting major UN offices in the Global South. The UN Office in Nairobi (UNON), the UN Environmental Program (UNEP) and the UN Habitat programs bring all manner of prestige and recognition to the country. And of course, there have been concerted attempts at moving the offices to some Western country. Most fortunately, African and Global South nations have been adamant about *not* moving the offices out of the country, illustrating the kind of support and hopefully respect that Kenya has commanded across the world.

UNEP and Habitat may not be the most glamorous UN offices, but there is a principle of fairness involved in locating them in Nairobi rather than in the capital of an advanced country in the west. Apart from the issues of security with regard to such weighty matters as nuclear energy and (non) proliferation, the UN does more work related to the Global South than to any other countries in the Global North: from peacekeeping to refugee (re) settlement to issues of food security. Kenya's and other nations' advocacy for the retention of the offices in Kenya is warranted and timely. These belong in the   Global   South.

Safe Haven: UNHCR, Refugees and Stateless Persons

Since the early 1990s, when the country known as Somalia became the first truly failed state, Kenya has hosted some of the largest refugee contingents in any country. Refugees have especially come from Somalia. Hosting refugees can be a challenge, especially when you have the same kings of citizens (Somalis) and therefore distinguishing between Kenyan Somalis and Somalia Somalis becomes almost a matter of chance.

African communitarianism does require that we extend kindness and also welcome those who are in need, and in this aspect, Kenya has been very welcoming. In fact, it has even welcomed refugees from as far afield as Burundi and the DRC.

While it has contributed the most significant numbers of refugees, Somalia is not the only country that has produced refugees who ended up in Kenya in droves. Modern day South Sudan has been another long-term source of refugees who have found refuge in Kenya, but this relationship is much more close and dates back to during the British colonial control of Kenya and its influence over the Sudan. In fact, some South Sudanese have grown up in Kenya and are, for all intents and purposes, Kenyan. The problem with South Sudan began almost immediately the country became independent in 1956 and has persisted to date. Even after South Sudan became the newest country, and conflict erupted, displaced South Sudanese refuges continued to flock south, most ending up in Kenya's capital.

Failed states produce conflict, instability, arms proliferation, banditry, and illegal trade, entry of contraband goods and sales of illegal firearms. These 'vices' then brook challenges to the host country, something that Kenya has experienced a lot particularly in the past 30 years. Indeed, one is torn between the African practice of kindness and generosity, and knowing that 'kikulacho ki nguoni mwako.' It is almost akin to picking up that poisonous snake encased in ice, and after it thaws out, it bites the unfortunate kind person with sub-optimal results. It is instructive for government to keep and even amplify vigilance even as it extends a temporary invitation to the suffering.

Refugees also regularly face food crises. Nothing is more likely to create food insecurity than conflict and the drought conditions found in the Horn of Africa, prompting these human movements and migration. Although Kenya had been the physical location of these camps, the UN through its various agencies such as the UNHCR has worked to help resettle the refugees, but many more have remained as conflict, instability and even terrorist attacks persisted in Somalia.

What is the future then of hosting many refugees so that they grow up in Kenya, while the country of origin appears less enthusiastic about fixing itself and claiming its population back so that they can begin rebuilding? Although Somalia exists as an outline of what is recognized as a state, it had failed to conduct itself as a Weberian nation for over 30 years. It is difficult to suggest that stateless persons in Kenya stem from the Somalia debacle, but it is unclear how the issue will resolve.

Perhaps one day, the Somali government will control more than the 6 blocks it occasionally controls and thus reclaim its citizens who are refugees from Kenya. But there is also the possibility that the refugee problem Kenya has will be part and parcel of the future, although if Africa unites as Nkrumah suggested, then the problem of refugees goes away.

UN: ICJ and Compliance.

Besides hosting several UN funds/programs, and serving on the UN Security Council (UNSC) as a non-permanent member three different times, Kenya is a partner to a number of initiatives that the UN has started and carries out around the continent and world, including for example, UNECA. But as suggested by some nugget of African wisdom, when two entities are in close proximity, the often rub each other the wrong way. This is the case with Kenya and Somalia (no surprise there), particularly on the issue of Kenya's maritime border. The disagreement eventually made it to the ICJ, which recently delivered its ruling in favor of Somalia, against Kenya.

The issue of borders, especially African ones, is challenging to settle especially today. Harkening back to the earliest days of African countries' independence, the OAU struggled with this question and decided to leave the borders as they were. This did nothing to solve the challenges of disagreement, or the very interesting decisions taken by the Europeans on frivolous grounds. One such example is the line that runs almost straight down from Lake Victoria (also, why do we still call it Lake Victoria?) to Tanga, with the exception of Mt. Kilimanjaro.

Rumor has it that Mt. Kilimanjaro was carved out of Kenya, because it had been given as a present to Kaiser Wilhelm II by his grandmother, Queen Victoria of the United Kingdom. It is still unclear how you give away a mountain in a foreign continent as a birthday gift – the thing is practically immovable, but also, it is not yours, and you sort of didn't ask the owners. But, these examples illustrate border considerations that newly independent African countries inherited and still struggle with. It is not clear that anything since the Cairo Declaration has actually made the issue of borders less contentious.

Even for a non-legal mind, the ICJ decision is most interesting. If one considers the maritime border between Kenya and Tanzania, it does not follow the land border line that culminates in a diagonal line down to Tanga from Kilimanjaro and further north-west. Instead, at the coast, it straightens out, and runs parallel to the Equator, eastwards. The Kenya/Somalia border, on the other hand, at the place where the two meet at the Indian Ocean, continues on a downward, diagonal south-east direction. Essentially, if the Kenya/Somali border and Tanzania/Kenya borders are drawn to their logical conclusion, Kenya's coastal waters are essentially a triangle.

In an attempt to perhaps increase Kenya's waters, the south-east angled line of Kenya's border was slightly adjusted northwards towards Somalia's 'territorial waters', but still, the logical end of the line still creates a triangle that defines Kenya's waters. There is absolutely no logic, or sense of fairness in the context of the ruling, as to why the Kenyan / Tanzanian (maritime) border goes east parallel with the Equator, and the Kenyan/Somalia border does not do the same, and continues its downward angled direction, severely constricting Kenya's share of the ocean.

It is almost as though Kenya is getting shafted in the entire process. Considering that Kenya only has 1,420 km of coastline, and Somalia has 3,333 km of coastline, it would seem that Somalia, especially having had so much support in reconstituting the state, and the uneven directions and decisions on borders, it would prize keeping the peace more than fighting over a few million liters of sea water. Then again, maybe that whole *Shifta* and 2011 invasion business still stings. The ruling and its justification sound almost like an invitation for Kenya to pick a fight with Tanzania and allege the same: if it is good for the goose, is it not supposed to be good for the gander too?

Kenya has thrown a tantrum every which way over the ICJ ruling, vowing to not abide by it, alleging that it will defend its territory (including that which the ICJ appeared to give to Somalia), all the way to include perhaps fighting Somalia a third time. While international law and decisions are important and must be respected, they also have to appear to be *fair*. The last word on the issue suggested that Kenya was getting ready to assert the Kenyan version of the US's Connally Amendment (paraphrased here to suggest that) Kenya will only comply with those ICJ decisions with which it agrees. Perhaps there is need for the UNCLOS to become more robust so that these many maritime disputes can be resolved, quickly, permanently.

This is decidedly selective diplomacy although Kenya appears to have a good case for disagreeing with the ruling. Kenya faces a delicate balancing act. On the one hand, it benefits a lot from the UN, from the UNON presence to other programs and funds. On the other hand, the mere fact that the UN is camping in its backyard is no reason for oppression. This is one of those items that require diplomacy between some of the most diplomatically oriented state/IGO duo.

Uarabuni: Work and Human Trafficking

it ought to smack of a bit of irony, that in a different part of this treatise, we argue that Kenya should interface with other countries so as to create avenues for the export of human resources, i.e., to get jobs abroad. The past several decades have seen a number of Kenyans travel to the Arabian Peninsula so as to obtain employment. While other positions get recruited – teachers, drivers, managers, etc., house work appears to attract the most workers. However, their lot especially working in Arabia has not always been one filled with great experiences.

It is utterly negligent for a country to abandon its people to such unfortunate and dehumanizing labor conditions. While one might argue that seeking employment – wherever – is a personal decision, sometimes these types of jobs can be like an undercurrent, just pulling individuals under and not letting them go, so that they become helpless and stuck in foreign lands, with the government appearing to not want to upset the Arabian nations even with those conditions..

Even worse, the contracts or the implementation thereof often makes the workers give up custody of their passports, which sounds like a form of slavery and a violation of human rights and workers' freedom to take up and give up employment. One wonders whether this is a matter that deserves a look by the ILO, the UN Human Rights Commission and other global human rights regimes, to determine if violations are occurring. But the ultimate responsibility for any actions and decisions lies with the Kenyan government.

Currently, for some reason, Kenya appears paralyzed and unwilling, unable or reticent to confront the recruiting agents, or the various governments in the countries where Kenyans exist and work in slavery and slave-like conditions. The near-constant heartrending stories of especially young women disappearing, dying, committing suicide, dying and being abandoned in the Arabian Peninsula, or being unable to return to Kenya are heart-breaking, as are their families' constant appeals. There is not

There is no more sacred responsibility for any government than the protection of a people denounced of private violence. Even if governments in the Middle East are unhappy at being confronted about the conditions of Kenyans in these countries, Kenya has got to exercise its responsibility over its citizens and their well-being. If it is unable to confront the conditions within the countries, perhaps it can revoke passports of individuals who have been taken against their will, but also investigate, prosecute, deport and otherwise punish the recruiting agents in Kenya. These are essentially the so-called low-hanging fruit.

At minimum, there should be no confiscation (or 'safe-keeping' of passports, or holding them hostage) by the labor agents or the employers. Granted, there is a possible loss of employment, but millions of people work on contract all over the world and do not have to give up IDs or passports as a condition of continued employment. The Kenyan government cannot be in the business of neglecting its citizens for whatever reason, money, good relations or otherwise.

To turn a blind eye on the happenings in the Middle East is essentially ignoring the clear and compelling evidence that there are violations of human rights, and likely human trafficking that occurs with the complicity of business concerns licensed by the Kenyan government. This is one of the areas in which a future government must take action, legislatively or by executive order. The protection of Kenyans is a government responsibility, here or there, and franchising out this role is just not part of what can be negotiable.

Regionalism, Regional Security and Neighbors

Kenya's neighbors are influential in the formation of its identity as a regional hub for peace, some because they lack it, and others because they are partners thereof. The past sixty years have been quite significant in how the country interacts with its neighbors, the influence it exerts on them and vice versa and the results of its engagement in the region. Besides Somalia and one instance of Amin's hyperbole, peace has persisted in the region.

Kenya's efforts are especially notable with regard to the conflicts in Somalia, in South Sudan and even far afield in Rwanda, Burundi and DRC. From deploying of peace-keeping troops, contribution of police forces to hosting transitional governments (especially in Somalia) to the hosting of peace talks and even refugees, Kenya has really demonstrated its importance in the Horn of African region and even farther abroad.

Participation in regional security issues, particularly aiding in the reconstitution of Somalia, the separation of South Sudan from Sudan and during the turbulent Amin rule, keeping a careful eye on Uganda have been in Kenya's **national security interest**. Kenya cannot expect or hope for security absent more or less similar conditions prevailing in the neighboring states. It is therefore invested, and should be a robust participant in ensuring peace, prosperity and security of its neighbors.

All manner of negative outcomes ensue from conflict and as such, containing refugees, arms proliferation, illicit trade and other similar issues is a most important strategy and goal for Kenya. As the previous three decades have shown, it is quite difficult to have peace and security when your neighbors are fighting and producing refugees into your territory, straining resources, security and a host of other things. It is important to continue being this next island in an often turbulent region. Every successive government should be committed to national security, but also to regional and continental security.

Expansion of the East African Community

Expansion of the East African Community (EAC), which is one of the oldest, and smallest of Africa's Regional Economic Communities (RECs) has been one of the major issues under deliberation over the past several years. While there are arguments for its expansion, including, for example, Rwanda's relatively significant success, there are also cautionary tales, including Burundi and South Sudan. Should the EAC expand to include Somalia and the DRC, as has been suggested and imagined?

Indeed, this is an intriguing question given that the EAC is one of the most advanced REC (at least in the region). Considering that these arguments are occurring in the context of whether the EAC and IGAD should merge, it is important to make the right decision. African IOs and IGOs often impose no cost whatsoever for membership and this has time and again shown to be a sub-optimal strategy. We should require more of any one or any country trying to join the regional economic communities such as EAC.

Kenya has also played a bigger role in more than the region: when Somalia collapsed and the age-old issue of piracy resurfaced and various navies deployed, it served as the location where some of the 'sea pirates' were held and tried, under various international agreements. In this case, it served a more global role, helping to combat and **mitigate the effects and impacts of piracy**. To wit, Kenya has been an important continental and global player, and it is necessary to continue playing this role, even as Kenya casts a larger shadow upon the international community and especially the African continent, and contemplates future possibilities such as whether it might be one of the African nations that could vie for membership to an African representative at the UN Security Council.

Secure installations and physical infrastructure

Terrorism has long been a feature of the contemporary world. Today, it is almost impossible to recall a time when a trip to the airport and onto a plane or train did not involve some combination of taking off shoes, belts, jackets, coins and all manner of other personal effects so as to go through security. There are good reasons to be careful and to secure the citizenry against these very real threats, and Kenya often appears to be attempting to do so. For the most part, around the world, we have come to accept these as the new 'normal' in the context of security apparatus, strategies and measures.

Kenya is no stranger to transnational terrorism, neither is it immune to terrorist attacks, either as a function of its own choices and arguably ill-advised sojourns abroad (in Somalia), or as a 'weak target' (target of opportunity) against foreign interests, as was the case with the bombing of the US Embassy in 1998 and the Kikambala Israeli charter jet incident in 2002. However, justified the reason was, by deploying troops into Somalia, Kenya ostensibly painted a massive target on its literal back, even as the nature, number, type and levels of violence of terrorist groups and violent non-state actors proliferated, got smarter with technology and got YouTube and Twitter, became more destructive, morphed and changed.

Although as a target for terrorist attacks Kenya may look like low-hanging fruit, there have been relatively few events of the catastrophic nature variety. However, there is never quite a feeling that Kenya is especially secure against possible future terrorist threats and attacks. Any trip to any decently-sized shopping mall brooks these fears and harkens back to Westgate. The gates at most malls are manned by security guards with likely no training in the kind of security terrorism would require, armed with a metal detector wand ostensibly to check for weapons, but lowly remunerated security officers are armed with nothing but confidence and a desperate hope that nothing terrible happens. As the machine-gun wielding, spraying-bullets-terrorists showed, courage in the face of a machine gun is followed by an almost always fatal outcome.

It is time for Kenya to deal better with terrorism. This includes securing its major installations better, but more importantly, articulating a national counter-terrorism strategy, one that includes how to deal with radicalization, and better trained officers to not only ferret out the future VNSAs. Citizens need to feel better secured while they frequent key installations and where citizens congregate. Also, if the attempted DHL Airbus shootdown in November 2003 has any lessons, even airports should be better secured – much better secured than the most interesting practice of security checks at the JKIA airport.

As Kenya continues to build new infrastructure, we need to also recognize that while we are not always a / the target, we host institutions, installations and important infrastructure that is always attractive to the VNSAs. At home, it is important to secure ports, transport facilities, flight paths and other places where terrorism might find targets. We should also educate the public and security officials in areas of critical importance that vigilance and *not* being corrupt is vital. Indeed, it is the essence of the national security of the Republic.

Chapter 13: Environmental Stewardship and Climate Change

ⒸⓈⓄⒸⓈⓄⒸⓈⓄ

1. Are Kenya's goals on combatting climate change too ambitious and costly to the country's economy?
2. Can Kenya, offering a 'Carbon Marketplace', invest in the sale of 'carbon credits' by planting billions of trees as a national tribute to its Nobel Prize winner Wangari Maathai?
3. How can Kenya decrease the environmental impacts of the changing climate particularly on its agriculture-dependent economy? (Might include irrigation and diversification)
4. Is Kenya prepared for the climate of the 2050s, and how can it continue to build climate/environmental resilience?

Introduction

In the old days of KBC, the government-funded series of radio and TV stations that were later mostly derisively referred to as the 'KANU Broadcasting Corporation,' if you had a TV, you were quite likely to see the 'weatherman' whose name we shall not repeat, for his own protection, go through the paces of the weather forecast. Then, an old adage suggested that no one perhaps told more 'untruths' than the weather–man; when he said it would rain, it did not; when he said it would be dry, and you left your umbrella home, you were totally drenched. You were probably also pretty mad at him for 'misleading' you.

The joke went on to argue that if the weather-man told you it would rain, prepare for the sun. For most of us, the weather is especially remarkable when it rains or when it does not (after all, over 60 percent of Kenyans are farmers), or when there is a sudden downpour in Nairobi and perhaps other cities, where it somehow appears to raise fares in an instant.

There are other elements of recognition of the effects of the weather on the citizenry, well-being, economy, daily activities, livestock, wildlife and the overall region. Even as the COVID-19 pandemic took hold across the world in the past two years, East Africa and the Horn of Africa have been in the grip of a locust infestation that keeps recurring, often with greater ferocity and in greater numbers.

There have been a total of 5 suspected waves and swarms of up to 2 billion locusts at a time, which take to the skies and land with great destruction of crops and pasture, massively impacting farming and pastoralism. Further, these swarms exacerbate the existing food crises that were especially imposed by the lockdowns and lack of government social supports. Weather conditions for a nation with a high reliance on agriculture for its GDP and employment not only impact productivity and wealth, but also the ability to work, and especially food security.

At the same time, the role that climate change is playing in changing overall global conditions is of great concern, and Kenya has been at the forefront of most efforts to consider how humanity is impacting and driving planetary changes, and to find solutions for this most pressing and potentially terminal issue. But even as it participates in global climate change accords and deliberations on how to ensure that climate change is contained and global warming likely stopped and reversed, it is not clear that Kenya has a very coherent, long-term strategy to combat climate change, even as it often undertakes programs that significantly impact the environment (e.g., outlawing the use of paper bags) while failing to discern the impact of motor vehicles on the environment.

On the other hand, climate change has the potential to change so much of Kenya's economy but also its heritage that is shared with the world. This is particularly the case with the wildlife situation. Perhaps this is impetus to do more, and more urgently, and to realize that Kenya's independent actions are not sufficient to secure especially the conditions necessary to thrive all across the different sectors. This then drives the need for more global action and advocacy, if for no other reason, for the animals that have little choice or impact on the climate.

Broadly, the world faces many climate and environmental challenges, and it is necessary to begin to take those actions that secure Kenya's future and that of the planet. The beauty and tragedy of living on this planet together is that we cannot just look the other way and not take actions, even if it's as simple as planting trees or increasing our advocacy, in order to heal the planet and make it livable for ourselves and our children. Has Kenya lived up to its obligations, and is it doing all that it can in order to ensure that this proposed future is secure?

UNEP, Rio 92, Paris Accords and Other Pacts

The United Nations Environment Program (UNEP), one of the few UN programs and funds that are not located within the Global North, found its location set to Kenya after the (first) Stockholm conference in 1972. This was an opportunity to take some pride in a global issue that, even though almost unrecognized then, at least its impact on humanity, would come to be as important as nuclear security – and influence the survival of species; not just ours, but of the entire planet.

Granted, having a HQ is not by itself a significant accomplishment, but it is a platform nonetheless. More needs to happen to deem UNEP and its location in Kenya a success, and some of it ought to stem from Kenya's own actions and advocacy considering the foregoing discussion. Rather curiously, as a percentage of the total 'negative climate actions' that others label pollution, Kenya's 'contribution' is almost negligible. But the estimated negative consequences of climate change on Kenya's economy are estimated at 3-5 percent of its GDP.[38]

According to the UNFCC, the agency that monitors climate change and actions to combat it, Kenya's contribution to global pollution is a paltry 0.1 percent, in line with most African and most other developing nations. In the post-Paris Climate Accords, in 2020, Kenya's initial commitment to reduce Greenhouse Gas (GHG) emissions was revised upwards from 30 percent to 32 percent by 2030, at a cost of US$62 billion[39] (or the equivalent of Kshs. 7.13 trillion).

This is more than twice Kenya's annual budget and $^2/_3$ of its annual nominal GDP as of 2020.[40] This is quite an expensive proposition, considering the general conditions in the country pitted against how much (or how little) damage the country is doing to the environment. Notably, the Ministry commits 13 percent to fight climate change and seeks 87 percent of the commitments from the international partners. There are global calls for especially the wealthy (and also mostly, industrial, polluting) nations to do more to meet such costs, but it is not clear that voluntary contributions can do this.

Kenya has been an active participant and an avid advocate in global environmental movement and climate change actions' strategies. It has participated at the various different global climate summits and actions, particularly Stockholm (1972), the World Commission on Environment and Development (1987), 'Rio (1992), GA Special Session on the Environment (1997), World Summit on Sustainable Development (2002), UN Conference on Sustainable Development (2012) and UN Sustainable Development Summit (2015).

The country has also strongly supported other related environmental strategies, conferences, workshops and even the United Nations Environment Assembly (UNEA), which was held most recently in 2019 in Nairobi Kenya. It also supports major climate actions such as the Paris Accords and the work of the Nobel Peace Prize-winning Intergovernmental Panel on Climate Change (IPCC).[41] How much its actual contributions make a difference is still unknown, but it is always important to have a seat at the table and from thence, find ways to create sustainable impact that goes beyond hosting UNEP.

As part of the participation in these international activities, Kenya has periodically articulated its proposed actions in compliance. UNFCC notes Kenya's 'ambitious' climate change achievement targets. One wonders: while it is useful to be a leader in combating climate change, what is the actual cost of climate change actions to the country especially if such actions impede industrialization for a country that is still far below most of the developed countries economically and otherwise?

Or is this simply signaling behavior, so that other developed nations might be shamed into doing more to combat climate change? The latter seems to never work, as the verbal football between the US, China and India has continuously shown. To the extent that Kenya pays for its climate change costs, it is going to be a most expensive undertaking for a country that contributes very little to the current circumstances, but suffer the consequences most seriously.

Nobel Prizes, 'Ukikata Mmoja' and Environmental Issues

One of Kenya's proudest moments — on an individual achievement basis (although we tend to claim these things), was the awarding of the Nobel Peace Prize to Wangari Muta Maathai, that erstwhile environmentalist who made planting trees her business, then ran for president and got about 15,000 votes before returning to saving the planet through carbon capture.

Founding the Greenbelt Movement in 1977, her objectives were listed as 'environmental conservation, building climate resilience and empower(ing) communities especially women and girls [and] foster democratic space and sustainable livelihoods.'[42] These, especially the fourth, was a tempestuous proposition, given that Kenya was a *de facto* one-party state, and in five years, would become a *de jure* one party state.

While the Nobel Prize Committee's specific reason for awarding the Prize was "for her contribution to sustainable development, democracy and peace,"[43] it took 27 years to get to that point. By then, Greenbelt had managed to plant more than 51 million trees and empowered 30,000 girls, neither of which was a small feat.

If only the Nobel Prize Committee knew how much trouble Wangari Maathai's trees caused in Kenya, including during the multiparty politics agitation. It is evident that long before the rest of the world recognized some of the more low-cost, effective strategies to capture GHGs, Wangari was onto something. But at the time, even the simple task of cleaning the Nairobi River (which Michuki subsequently managed to do) before it went back to that dark, likely highly poisonous effluent) seemed like a Herculean task.

We should give credit where it is due. Even as the world was beginning to meet to begin to deal with climate change, Kenya had already started moving in the same direction. Daniel Arap Moi pledged to 'follow in the footsteps of Kenyatta,' but also began implementing public infrastructure projects that included attempting to deal with the climate.

In the mid-to-late 1980s, even as the political space was becoming highly constrained and two unlikely allies – Wangari and President Moi – were both encouraging citizens to plant trees, the popular 'ukikata mmoja, panda miwili' (when you cut down one, plant two trees) philosophy was alive and well. Chiefs occasionally raised a stink in the event that some hapless citizen cut down trees without a permit, but for a country that is primarily fed through wood-fire cooking, it was not possible to strictly enforce the idea that folks could not cut down trees for wood.

Then-president Moi did attempt to encourage the planting of trees, including in the Nyayo Tea Zones. Some of the relics of this program can be seen near 'Soko Mjinga' near Kijabe. For all the negative things that they may have done, past leaders have occasionally tried to safeguard the environment. They have no choice: majority of their population depends on it for farming (food) and economic well-being (crops sales).

Perhaps there is a lesson in all this. Given that trees trap a lot of carbon dioxide and are often considered to be good 'banks' for carbon dioxide, which is one of the primary contributors to GHG emissions, Kenya should begin to plant trees like its future depends on it, so as to establish a **carbon marketplace for emissions 'dumping' to combat climate change and environmental degradation** – basically, wealthy nations would pay us to plant trees (which is also good for rainfall) in a form of trade-off. It is a system that benefits all.

Plastic Bags and Environmental Cleanups

Kenya has already demonstrated the kind of zeal that can get it to do those things that are hard, but necessary. The country banned the use of plastic bags in 2017, but it is now observed that single-use plastics, especially of the polyethylene terephthalate (PET)[44] variety, are literally choking the country.

As is often the case, Kenya's decisions have little rhyme or reason: it bans single-use plastics, but in the same moment, continues to allow single-use plastic. Today, the disposal of face-masks faces little to no direction, and as the world has found out, humans may be avoiding contagion through mask use, but the sea is choking full of the largely non-biodegradable, sometimes flimsy, locally-made cloth masks.

There is probably a greater likelihood of dealing with this issue if the bottles had deposits attached to them although this may be seen as a non-tariff barrier to trade, or if a robust recycling program was in place, including the provision of recycling bins in public. But there is also the question of educating Kenyans as to what is recyclable, and what is not. For example, the flimsy cloth bags that replaced the plastic bags are rarely recycled, creating a new problem similar to the 'old problem.'

In addition, one of the 'replacement' products for the paper bag was the actual paper-version of the paper bag. These are made by cutting down wood, which is sort of the worst possible solution to a terrible problem. Perhaps encouraging the use of woven, multiple-use bags, or providing the same for a small fee, would resolve most of both of those issues.

Government must also ensure that besides **encouraging recycling, single use–plastics** are **outlawed** just like paper bags.

As cities go, Nairobi is nowhere near clean – and neither are most of the other cities in Kenya. There is litter, refuse, stinky alleys, trash on streets, dust, smoke, smog, noise, vehicle emissions and all manner of life-threatening environmental and other hazards. It is unlikely that Nairobi gets anyone to clean it (sweep, wash the streets) as some cities do. Environmental care is not just about trees and not using coal.

It is also about noise levels, city planning and organization, how traffic moves (or mostly, does not move), the rabid overcrowding in residential areas and streets, trash discarded in the streets and other issues. Here, Kenyan cities need to do more. At present, 'doing more' may be much more tempered by the empowerment of the counties, allowing for more revenue generation so that they can increase their services to citizens and be able to offer 'differences' from other counties. Cleanups of cities, streets, streams, emissions and effluence must become a priority as an environmental undertaking.

Climate: Solar vs. Coal Powered Power Plants

The past decade or so has seen Kenya flirt with the idea of investing in the use of coal, nuclear energy and other more dubious sources of power. We ought to be cognizant of global trends, including the reality that most countries are mostly abandoning especially nuclear energy, while the use of coal is also in decline, with most deeming it 'dirty' fuel (alongside with hydrocarbons-based fuels, especially when it burns.

Further, digging up coal procures all kinds of health conditions, such as 'black lung disease.' It is not clear why we would want to invest in dirty fuels such as coal, oil and in nuclear energy, especially if it is likely that some environmental accident might occur. HEP, on the other hand, is less dirty, but considering the levels of rainfall that Kenya gets, it is necessary to look to other possibilities and sources.

Kenya has an abundance of essentially free energy sources, i.e., solar. For most of the year, year round, the sun rises between 6:20 and 6:41 p.m. and repeats during the evening when it sets. The use of solar power in Kenya is still on a very small scale: some homes have solar power panels which mostly power bulbs and TVs, but expanding the use of such solar power facilities to cooking and other household needs will improve Kenyans' lives, without any corresponding degradation of the environment – except perhaps with the disposal of the solar panels. Indeed, the lack of a cohesive solar power strategy indicates how remiss we have been, particularly given the potential of solar power.

The next government should review the energy policy of the entire country, and while we might cheer the discovery of oil in Turkana, it is most important that the government **develop an energy strategy that prioritizes solar power in small and localized grids** powering homes, schools, small enterprises and factories, while developing it for use by car battery manufacturers. This requires changes in current energy policy.

Solar power is probably Kenya's greatest find that has not been well-exploited. Kenya ought to invest in nothing less than the moon-shot for solar power: find ways to create powerful generators that turn all that sun into electrical energy. Some of the strategies that can be used are self-evident.

New **houses**, for private, residential occupation, private businesses or for government use, should be **built with solar panels installed on roofs**. The government should also require that each ministry begin to transition from electrical power to solar power, because they can create localized power grids without running afoul of legislation governing the roles of KPLC and KenGen in power generation and in power distribution.

Further, the government should give much more leeway to private SMEs to install **standalone, localized solar power grids** even if deems that requiring them to utilize at least 10–25 percent of their power needs drawn from the HEP and Geothermal generation capacities will help offset some of the potential loss of clients and revenue, but also reduce the cost of manufacturing and ensure that there is reliable power supply.

This will leave the two SOEs to focus on generation and distribution of power to citizens. At the same time, it will allow schools, which are supposed to be centers of innovation, to secure their own power sources. The upside that will be created through the use of electrical power to power homes and schools will produce such a boon in production that any losses would be offset by higher usage. There are other areas of potential and future use of solar including manufacture of electrical cars and electrical-powered trains.

Youth and Climate Change

Climate change will affect youth especially significantly, and it is necessary to ensure that there a future, an environment and regulated climate in their future. That they are better represented in the unemployment and under-employment rolls is important, because the carbon marketplace proposal has the potential to provide employment while giving the youth opportunity to be stewards of the climate.

To date, Kenya's youth have not been involved at any significant level, and/or been at the forefront of these proposals for change or in strategies to deal with climate change, even though they are the most likely to be affected by future climate change – whether we arrest the warming, or re-green the planet. It is necessary to leverage youth enthusiasm and energy to create the future environment that will allow the planet to survive.

Youth have already shown that they are the future of climate change. The erstwhile teen, Ms. Greta Tintin Eleonora Ernman Thunberg, the no-nonsense, world—leader—condemning Swedish has unequivocally made the case for better global climate stewardship, observing rather correctly, that the youth will inherit the earth from this generation, that they have the greatest stakes in the health and well-being of the planet, and that they are willing to fight for the right to exist into the future. It is enlightened thinking to lead to better programs.

Some of the proposals included here are those that allow youth both the opportunity and funding to pursue programs and policies that contribute to the future. But they also have the capacity to be the source of programs and products as would be useful economically, now and in future, and procure the skills needed for good environmental stewardship. They include such proposals as competitions to design miniature solar power grids, planting trees in the 'carbon marketplace' strategy, reducing the overall waste generation and emissions, and related activities.

Regional Challenges and Future Opportunities

By virtue of its physical location, Kenya has no choice but to undertake such actions as assure that it can continue to combat environmental and climatic conditions, such as the locust infestation, drought and the effects of periodic climate changes such as El Nino and La Nina. By working with regional and global organizations with better capacity for **monitoring, forecasting and climatic conditions and climate change surveillance,**

Kenya can respond better to the challenges that come its way. In this context, IGAD and FAO are especially important partners. The country would also benefit greatly if it invested greatly in directed environmental actions, such as decreasing dependence on rain for most of the pastoral and agricultural activities undertaken in the country.

One of the future proposals for this or the next administration is to create programs that can reduce the begging and encourage investment in programs that are helpful to both the planet and the country. It is important to create a **'carbon exchange'**, to utilize abundant labor in Kenya to **plant trees in the millions to billions,** for and on behalf of especially the wealthy countries, which will then use that as a trade opportunity, **purchasing credits to offset carbon emissions** and meet both national and global goals for combating climate change.

Not only will this contribute to the global good, it will also help Kenya's overall climatic conditions by hopefully attracting more rain and thus increasing the overall rainfall, even though we agree that we ought to utilize technology to ensure that we are becoming more efficient at agriculture. To

Kenya has some command of a major global environmental platform, through which it can **command** and **advocate for global climate actions, i.e., UNEP**. It is evident that the problem of the Global North's domination of global affairs, including those of climate, is unlikely to much change, even as it continues to affect the whole world. In this, the country can and ought to be one of the global leaders into a vision of the oft touted reality: there is no 'Plan(et) B.'

Climate change is one of those global issues that occasion Extinction Level Event types of outcomes. Crop failures, hunger, drought, rising seas, changing climate patters, poor agricultural production and a less hospitable planet affect us all, now, but especially significantly in future. Kenya has no choice but to utilize its platform to leverage its existential interests and to advocate, through its critical UNEP megaphone and its own climate experiences, the necessity of this planet surviving. That, or make fast friends with Elon Musk, for when he finds a new planet.

Chapter 14: Society, Culture and Traditions

ͻ෴ͻ෴ͻ෴

1. What socio-cultural traditions are especially harmful to some members of the Kenyan collective and how can we modify them to fit modernity?
2. Should government more forcefully intervene in containing the more radical, human-rights violating socio-cultural traditions found within some communities?
3. Do socio-cultural traditions, practices and beliefs impact all Kenyans the same way or are some society's members more significantly affected? (Women, girls definitely are)
4. How can we properly, progressively and most productively integrate socio-cultural traditions into modern Kenyan society? What do we need to keep and what should we lose?

Our Cultural Traditions: The Good, The Ugly, The Future

There is a Swahili adage that rings true – maybe it is – that, 'Mwacha mila ni mtumwa' (translation: those without culture are, essentially, subjects and at worst, slaves of other cultures). There is another saying from a different society, one that alleges that "the dinosaurs became extinct because they could not adapt." Or because they didn't learn history or something about a big rock hitting earth. Whichever it was, culture and traditions are an essential element of human expression, they are quite important, and the importance is both self-evident and worth highlighting, particularly with regard to how culture influences the conduct of régimes and societies e.g., Kenya's.

Sociocultural traditions have given us (and other cultures, societies and nations) many things of beauty and appreciation. They give us the ability to communicate and understand each other (through language, shared or learnt). Culture gives us identity, different elements of our existence that we learn, celebrate, modify and discard (e.g., weddings, initiation, bride wealth payment, dowry, etc.)

Culture also gives us identity, whether it's through names that have meaning (e.g., those who are named after ancestors, heroes, seasons or events) or through membership of the broader class of age-sets. Culture gives us various events to celebrate and individuals to admire and to revere (as heroes, both men and women). It gives us things to do on a periodic basis, through national holidays and celebrations, and creates experts at these different activities. Culture is this'll us part of what, who we are, rather than something outside of us.

While there are many positive things about culture, there are others that are detrimental, and make little to no sense, and only continue just because it's what we have been doing. Some of these cultural traditions have been overtaken by time, by technology, religion, science, human rights and most of all, by reason. As such, when they continue, they harm individuals and society, serve no useful purpose and diminish us as human beings. Such traditions include for example, FGM.

Traditions such as FGM serve no discernible useful purpose beyond depriving a woman of the right to choose and enjoy different experiences, bodily autonomy, freedom from pain and the right to not be disadvantaged by gender or decision-making on the assumption that FGM reduces personal sexual pleasure, among other reasons. The silence that exists around African culture, particularly with all things related to sexuality, also rarely allows for thoughtful deliberation on the merits of those things that people do and hold dear, even where scientific evidence might suggest that their existence and practice is detrimental.

We have often been quick to embrace foreign ideas and even foreign technology and some aspects of other cultures. For example, a lot of the music playing on our airwaves by local musicians is often indistinguishable from the music of the west, while we have adopted a lot of their sports and other elements, including religion – considering that most African societies had some form of religion and/or deity. With the latter, upon the mid–1800s start of the arrival of European missionaries, we adopted elements of their religions and beliefs. More contemporarily, we accept the technology that is cell-phones, and TV, but we stick stubbornly to some of our traditions.

It would be most ironic, were it to happen, for a Maasai father to be negotiating dowry within early marriage for his daughter using a cell-phone. Contemporary art and media through programs such as the longest-running *The Bold and the Beautiful,* or its counterpart, *Days of our Lives,* and the now-long gone *La Mujer de mi Vida* speak of great love but we won't even walk parallel to each other with our significant others. We recognize modernity and its significant benefits and changes, but continue to pay and collect dowry even though salient reasons for which dowry was collected no longer exist.

As *the* Kenyan nation, it is necessary to take inventory of the nation that we are, what we do and how we deliberate especially the thorny issues that affect the most important and disadvantaged among us. We should, have to come to consensus on the future things that are acceptable and the ones that are not, whether they are part and parcel of what constitutes our future or not. For Kenya is a multi-ethnic nation, and thus has those issues governed by both constitutional law and sociocultural traditions and occasionally, religious practices.

This necessarily makes it challenging to agree on certain things (for example the outlawing of FGM), because they have cultural connotations however vile we find them. But that only makes the role of the state more challenging, because it becomes necessary to agree that such practices as FGM and early child marriages are decidedly un-African and against the law, and also violate women's human rights.

Science, Knowledge and Adaptations to Cultural Traditions

Every piece of knowledge, science and research tells us that some traditions are especially harmful to either parts or the whole of society. That it is also perpetrated by women upon women (or girls) is a most unfortunate and disturbing reality. FGM is not just a violation of women's basic human rights; it is also inherently dangerous health-wise and has been associated with difficulty and even death, during childbirth.

As a country, we have progressively decreased maternal mortality, and the probability that we would increase it again by continuing with practices that are clearly harmful to women just so we can say they are 'initiated' is something that we need, and ought to shun. FGM is one of those long-lived traditions that have been long overtaken by time, that has no place in modern society, and one and that ought to no longer exist today.

What traditions need to stay and which ones need to go? It is probably inopportune to appeal to science, to suggest that those traditions and beliefs that are not supported by science should probably be left by the wayside, but culture can be a deeply personal thing, a thing not of science, but of history, ancestry, practice, and even fear – fear that any disruptions will bring about untold misery and evil.

Questionable beliefs and irrational fears arising from traditions and beliefs are not necessary a Kenyan thing. Even in developed societies, there are elements of these beliefs that are not grounded in science. A couple of them include a black cat crossing the road ahead of a motorist (you should probably turn around back to the origin of the journey), stepping on a crack (it is said to break your mom's back), walking under a ladder (not sure what happens) and opening an umbrella indoors (not sure what happens either).

At the same time, there are clearly harmful practice and beliefs. It is one thing to believe that a black cat is as evil as anything one might encounter (consider how murderers might navigate that sentiment), or the proposition of walking under a ladder – an individual might never have the need for any of these instances, and even if they did, they would not get them excommunicated and shunned by their communities, but something like FGM has actual consequences.

And it is not just FGM. The proposition that young, school-going girls are married off to (sometimes, often) older men with an exchange of dowry is also a most distressing reality. It is also a reality that exists, despite its needlessness. There are other ways to obtain dowry, and even if one were cynical, they might consider that life expectancy in some communities provides little to no assurance that the girl will even make it to marriage.

Because early child marriages and practices such as FGM are part and parcel of cultural traditions in certain societies, and especially FGM is actually harmful, even occasionally lethal in its performance and later during childbirth, there is science and knowledge that supports its abolition. And if the objective is 'initiation' into adulthood, it is useful, even obligatory, to find other ways of 'initiating' young women into their society, if this is necessary (we could absolutely have a debutante dance of sorts, or those simulated ceremonies that have taken to being performed without any of the gory stuff and cutting.

Kenyan communities have a duty to both the past, to consider it in the context of history, modernity and the future of their members. They have an obligation to evaluate what they do, why they do it, and what else they can do as pertains to the culture, its adaptations and excisions. We need to ensure that any initiation that goes on does not continue to harm girls and women, or in the worst case scenario, potentially turn lethal. We owe it to all the women and girls whom we purport to love and whom we have an obligation to protect.

Continuity is Change

The idea that 'change is the only constant thing' is well worn, but probably true. There are few things that are untouched by change, even the Terracotta soldiers or the Egyptian pyramids and their contents, even when they were designed to be unchanging. But mankind's propensity and capacity for change is probably his most important t value, otherwise he would still be scratching cave walls and hunting and gathering.

Even those areas of human endeavor where change appears to be practically impossible do go through change. Culturally, change can be difficult. Usually, older members of the community serve as guardians and gatekeepers of cultural beliefs and practices, and as research shows, we become more conservative in old age, and are likely to support the status quo.

Consider some Kenyan societies in the central and western regions. For the longest time, the idea of having twins was frowned upon, with the twins being considered a 'bad omen' or equivalent. It is alleged that folks from the central province would leave such twins out in the forest, to a fate that might include death by a scavenging wild animal.

There was no scientific evidence procured that twins actually caused evil, or the mechanism that would have ensued. Today, we know that any such 'evidence' was most likely coincidence. We have since clearly evolved to a place of believing that twins are more of a double blessing, not a bad omen. If we consented to, and eventually changed and co-exist with this particular question of twins, how can we then argue that it is *not* possible to change some of our cultural traditions and beliefs? Methinks it is not, no matter how challenging the idea of change can be, and no matter how much resistance we find in those entrenched beliefs in the community.

As a country, and as groups of constitutive communities, we must believe that change is possible and that we *are the essence of change*. Change is constant: in 2000, few, if any of us, had a mobile phone. Today we are subscribed at almost 110 percent. We had scant idea that your (then-non-existent) mobile phone can also serve as your bank, or that you can conduct business with the government on eCitizen efficiently.

We did not anticipate that we can have a proliferation of radio stations right and left, or that we might be in a Zoom environment, teleworking from home due to a global pandemic. There are many things we do not foresee, but adapt to, accept, leverage and even get quite creative with. 'Change is the only constant thing' is not an exaggeration. Now, as a nation, we must be brave and look to the future, discarding those things that are unhelpful thereto.

Sociocultural Attitudes

Are we at all sold on the proposition that all men are created equal, and have the same God-given abilities – except perhaps the superiority of women who are actually able to procreate and eject whole humans from their body, something that might kill stronger men? Many cultures are perhaps unwittingly discriminatory in ways that are especially unhelpful in creating a more egalitarian society with respect for women's rights.

Their practices diminish our overall experience as human beings, decrease the collective productivity that we can achieve as individual micronations and as the republic that is Kenya. We not only violate the human rights of some members of the society, but we even violate Euclid's Common Notions that were first discovered almost millennia ago. Yet some of the most important people in our individual lives are women: mothers, wives, sisters, daughters. Investing in the necessary work to treat women equally is long overdue and calls for cultural solutions.

It is perhaps unhelpful to re-hash the questions surrounding the role of women in Kenyan society, which was previously widely considered under Gender Equity. However, we acknowledge that women's (not) holding leadership positions of power is also a function of our cultures, and cultural problems are most often resolved through cultural responses.

In most of our cultures, even some of our cultural traditions target women and discriminate against them, in ways that are harmful the self-esteem and health, as we saw with FGM. The invisibility of women in our cultures is also something to be concerned about, and to attempt to reverse. Besides the disenfranchisement, even in the raising of families, while they arguably do most of the work and we take the credit for it, treatment of women leaves much to be desired.

In most of our communities, women are not seen or heard. It is joked that men from the Central Province introduce their wives thus: 'huyu ndiye wa kwangu' (tr: this is the one from my home). There is no sense that the two are building, or have built a home together. Many communities point to culture as an explanation of why they cannot do things that bring about equality, such as inheritance.

It appears then that some cultures exclude the full participation of women and girls simply because they are women and girls, not because they have the inability to excel and improve humanity. Considering that they give life to humanity, it is time that we consider and eliminate those barriers that stand in the way of the full participation of women in Kenyan – especially political – life, and make us all better.

But: Culture Can Be a Good Thing

Despite the clear and obvious weaknesses that sometimes culture has on our treatment of members of our society, it has its upsides, which can be leveraged for the good of society, for the learning and teaching opportunities, and to create a better country and society. How many of us, when we take a trip somewhere, want to see the sights, hear the sounds, experience the tastes and get to know the inhabitants of a place?

As Kenya's domestic tourism continues to grow – even with the ever-present threat of COVID-19 and its mutations, the opportunities for international travels and tourism to Kenya continue to expand exponentially – and we know that post-COVID cabin fever will bring many a traveler our way; travelers who have also come to realize that life is short. It is not the same, seeing a place from pictures, YouTube or even VR.

Plus, they may not have found a way to taste food from a distance yet. When we really think about it, culture is at the heart of tourism across the globe.

Consider the following places and events: New Orleans' Mardi Gras. Carnivals all over the US. Cinco de Mayo. The Wagner Festival. The running of the bulls in Pamplona, Spain. SXSW. The Kenya Schools Music Festival. These and many more have come to be well regarded. It is because they celebrate the culture of a place (and sometimes, the beer and food). If there is a place with culture and (some people argue, bland food), it is Kenya, and we should find ways to hopefully not only celebrate these but also, share them with the world.

Amongst the most celebrated cultures, there are often mixtures of performance and architecture; one contemplates the beauty of the Dance of a Thousand Hands at the 'Temple of Shin Din' and recognizes that cultural, culinary and performance tourism can be very lucrative as a source of foreign exchange. And Covid, unlike Bond's diamonds, is not forever. Kenya can indeed create a 'Bomas in the Streets' – 'Bomas Mtaani,' where we bring the culture of the peoples of Kenya to the streets for the world to partake of.

Perhaps this section should have started with, 'we know how to find the next Lupita.' Imagine if we took each Kenyan community and asked them to prepare half a day of any mix of song and dance, poetry, story-telling, riddles, wise-sayings and the like (we could even literally craft a Jeopardy! competition in there). And we haven't even talked about food!

Of course, any of these proposals require the careful involvement of, for example, the Ministry of Health. Imagine if we then recorded the same and used the myriad avenues available to us such as social media to advertise our offerings. And because we have creative youths and the rest of the world cannot always travel, creating a paid virtual experience. In fact, one might consider that the opportunities are endless, including of virtual marathons and such.

Officially, the 43 communities would take us to a most glorious three weeks of song and dance. Adding school performances from the music and drama festivals adds more days to this street carnival. Now, since we are in the six-member East African Community (EAC), we could absolutely invite our East African brothers so that they showcase their own societies, and perhaps even those who are in other RECs such as IGAD.

And while we do not intend to Balkanize and or tribalize Tanzania, we would like to think that they too have cultural experiences they would like to share. An invitation to our brethren to the south, as well as those from other countries in the region, would be a boon for both culture and good relations. The formats of participation might include purchasing tickets for the entire experience, for daily or flex attendance, or for elements thereof. Of course, we could decide to only do the festival in the afternoon (after all, people probably need to work).

On the last day of the festival, we should cap it with a first Running of the Great Kenyan Marathon (which strangely doesn't exist yet, even though we dominate some of the most important marathons around the world). In fact, while we are at the planning and proposing element of this, we could absolutely impress upon the WRC that the Safari Rally portion of the competition should occur about the same time, and preferably when it's colder in the northern hemisphere

This would allow for vacationers out of the colder reaches of Europe and Americas to come to Kenya and behold these cultural items and our decidedly (to be impressive) spectacle. Of course, it helps if we as Kenyans can begin to see the big picture and get better at organizing things efficiently and effectively, so that the types of scandals that rock FK, KPL and even the Rio Olympics do not taint an event of such massive national, potentially global importance. It would decidedly be one of the first and perhaps only ones across Africa.

Perhaps in all these performances, we might have occasion for talent scouting (hence Lupita) But even if we didn't find a *new* Lupita, we would still give the whole world an experience of a lifetime. We would have the opportunity to expand business opportunities (food, curio, travel) and increase sales of Kenya's commodities. In fact, this would also allow for other sectors to show-case their products including agriculture (tea, coffee, flowers) and to potentially procure new opportunities for exports. There is an absolute win-win outcome.

On a broad and global scale, we would have the opportunity to shine a light to Kenya's experiences and especially earn the country billions from other sources of tourism other than wildlife, even though this might definitely be one of the critical elements of the festival. But we would also have the opportunity to expose our fellow Kenyans to other ideas, so that we improve their ability to interact, especially the younger generations, to opportunities that might otherwise not exist, especially of the preservation of culture.

Cultural Tolerance or Cultural Colonialism

It is convenient, but probably lazy, to just pick up a made-in-India soap opera, stick it with some local language dialog, and market it as the newest arrival in entertainment. Whereas it may provide some entertainment (my own family is firmly hooked to *kumkum bagghya*, correct spelling unknown), it does nothing for growing our own local entertainment scene, or perhaps for cultural vibrancy. And some of that material that is broadcast, if correctly translated, is absolutely offensive as general broadcast materials especially if children are watching. In fact, here, it seems as though the KFC has dropped the ball on censorship.

Production of good quality dramas and soap operas is probably quite pricey, but we cannot content ourselves with only foreign products that may or may not relate to our local conditions. And while art is just that – art, we have to be more discerning about what art we are indeed exposing our communities to and whether it is compatible with our values. We need to support, encourage and build local content so that even the values that are infused by media are compatible with our goals as a nation - and no, this does not mean censorship, just more local content relative to foreign programming.

In the same vein, and despite the exponential growth of *Afrosinema*, it is important to think about what kinds of production are made, what they depict and especially the messages that they transmit to Africa and abroad, about Africa to those abroad, and whether we are privileging the best of what Africa can offer. Not being a fan of Nollywood, the few films and docudramas one sees on TV are heavily infused with those assumptions that paint us in some of the worst light

It has been beyond time to get rid of the stereotypical half-naked cast members wrapped in *shukas*, with dramas showcasing or including instances of voodoo-magic and story-lines that suggest that we have not outgrown some of our unflattering pasts as painted by others. We need to remember that in some parts of the world, Africa is (still) considered a country and so Kenyans cannot escape being tagged with the 'other' storylines that are unbelievably simplistic, misleading and not representative of who we are as a people and as a nation.

Tech, Modernity and Lessons not Learned

It is not easy to determine, on a national scale, what types and specific cultural beliefs we should, or if we should even change them. An inventory of each community's future can let them determine what they are doing that has been overtaken by time, that is unnecessary, harmful, and degrading and needs to go. FGM is clearly one of those practices. Dowry is questionable. The notion that a man can marry many wives is currently legal, but under a deservedly moral assault since it is clearly traditional but discriminatory.

The removal of the six lower front teeth has become a rarity rather than the normal practice, on account that we have found different ways of dealing with one of the purported reasons, lock-jaw. Wife inheritance, while rumors are rife with the idea that it happens, has lost much of its allure since the country's independence. It is clear then, that countries and societies can emphasize certain things, frown on others and even discourage the performance of some traditions.

Culture is broad, and it has both wonderful and also less than pleasant tenets. Kenya is a multi-national state (national, because it comprises of many mini-nations) that must all live together and figure out how to create harmony without losing the identities of the groups that make it so. We do need to find the balance of who we will be, celebrate all the good (and food, according to the text editor) that is in us, building a stronger, better, more culturally-celebratory nation.

But we must also pledge to ourselves, our daughters, sisters and even our sons and brothers and fathers, that we have an obligation to change with the times, to make the tough choices of not pretending that all of our cultural traditions, beliefs and practices are okay and that they must never be discarded, lest that make us 'watumwa.' Let's have a national dialog about what kind of culturally appropriate country we would like to bequeath unto our future countrymen and women.

Chapter 15: New Paths on Selected Issues

ଔଷୠଔଷୠଔଷୠ

1. Why have we not prioritized the building of a Mombasa-Nairobi-Kisumu dual-carriage 60 years after liberation?
2. Why can't we pay workers on time, twice a month?
3. Why do we all get to work at 8, take lunch at 12 and leave work at 5 to get into long *Matatu* queues? What does a dynamic work setting with staggered hours look like?
4. Why does dropping out of school before KCSE sound a death knell to the educational hopes of most Kenyans?
5. Do we need, or have a drug policy and if so, what is it?
6. Why do we still have colonial names for Lake Victoria? Can we rename the Thames after Obama or Mandela?
7. Are Kenyans too dependent on the government? Is Kenya both a nanny state and a bandit nation?
8. How can we end the number plate fraud long perpetrated against Kenyans in the vehicle registration process?

Introduction

There are elements of Kenyan society that could use a bit of improvement, and that do not warrant their own chapter or expansive explanations. However, it is our view that making changes in these issue areas will be a most welcome thing so that Kenyans do not only do things because that is how we found them being done, but because *it makes sense* to do things a certain way, although as history has shown, change is one of the most challenging things to embrace, and 'this way' almost always seems to be the better way.

Take the 'privilege' of driving. We have driven on the left side of the road (or we pretend to – really, we are usually all over the road) because it was a concept that we inherited from the British as part of the colonial 'package,' rather than because there was some inherently good argument for driving on the left side of the road. Therefore, we purchase vehicles with a steering column on the right side. Since we do not manufacture cars, this almost leaves us with no choice but to import cars mostly from Japan and the UK despite other major car markets and sources such as the US (and the US will likely not just make vehicles with LHD just so that they can export them to Kenya). And so we lock ourselves out of a major source of cars.

Why can't we allow the imports of LHD vehicles or even change the side on which we drive? After all, more modern vehicles have cameras that probably do a better job than humans. There is nothing inherently useful about driving on the left side; it was just what they did. Although to change driving sides might be wading into a beef that began with pilgrims, maybe we ought to ask more questions about why.

Bottleneck Infrastructure

Whereas infrastructure has been especially deliberated upon previously, there is another of those most confounding historical – even ongoing occurrences – that should be rectified in the shortest time period possible. Successive governments have invested some infrastructure development projects, building highways within about 50 kilometer radius of Nairobi: to Thika, Limuru and most recently, Kitengela and Athi River.

Perhaps the worst element of Kenya's infrastructure is that we do not have a highway in the most obvious places: between Nairobi and the western reaches of the country. Even when a train was built, it is active between Nairobi and Mombasa. Not to rain on the southeastern region of Kenya, but in terms of population, West-North-West has far more people, and worse roads and railways than the more sparsely populated south-east.

As a matter of urgency, the government should conceive, implement and rapidly commence a project to build a two-lane highway from Mombasa through Nairobi to Busia/Kisumu, to the urgent exclusion of all other projects including extension of the SGR railway. While it is the case that hindsight is 20/20, this ought to have been the very first major infrastructure project that the 1963, independence government should have undertaken. There is perhaps a variety of reasons why the first, third and fourth governments did not do such projects.

But even if the reasoning was that leaders were building infrastructure close to their residencies (as Mobutu did with the airport in Gbadolite and as some suppose for the international airport in Eldoret), the second government did not build infrastructure where it would have made sense, although it would have benefitted it, if only to make travel between Nairobi and Baringo and his other concerns much easier. Instead, an international airport was built in Eldoret. This is flummoxing.

Most who consider the pros and cons of the international airport agree that it serves little of the international purpose for which it was allegedly constructed, given that it is ultimately more expensive and time consuming, time-wise, particularly given that on landing, one would have to then commence a 6-hour road-trip over a terrible A104 pretending to be a highway, and the importance of the town itself. In fact, it absolutely makes no sense to fly to Eldoret if your final destination is Nairobi or Dar es Salaam, or if your connecting flight leaves from Nairobi.

It is necessary for the next government to undertake the construction of a dual-carriage highway between Mombasa and Western Kenya as the *first* priority and as a matter of national importance, perhaps even as a matter of national security. It is the case that today, high ranking politicians can fly their helicopters on our dime from Nairobi to any of the areas west, but the rest of us waste billions of man-hours and productivity just sitting in traffic jams particularly past Limuru, not to even considering the amount of pollution we are putting out there.

Old School Practices: Pay for Work Done

In regular discourse, 'old school' can be a good thing, but in this case, it is not. One of perhaps the most disturbing aspects of formal employment in Kenya is the way we work (reporting to work) and get paid (if we do, for the work we do). After people have done one whole month of work, they then have to wait until nearly the 5th of the *next month* to get paid. It is unclear why this is the practice, or what kind of negative implications that the waiting has on the workers.

One suspicion is that being late with the salary discourages the workers, so that they are less incentivized to work, which contributes to poor service to the public. A human resources department ought to recognize this, and even though this may be the practice, there is nothing to suggest that doing what has been the practice is necessarily a good thing. Neither is it quite a suggestion that precedent should not be changed.

Among some of the improvements that we propose and that we would implement would be for more employers to commit to pay employees on time, without that three-to-five day lag, or they would then have to pay interest, because at some point, we have to start exacting a cost on those that do not do the right thing (your workers already worked). Of course, the government would be the lead on this, including publication of pay schedules at the very beginning of the year.

The commitments include a **biweekly pay by direct deposit, with published pay** schedules for the year. For those employers and their employees who find that they are unable to work with the biweekly schedule, a weekly or monthly pay schedules with the same publication of the schedules early in the year would be required. At no time should pay spill into the next month, for an individual who has done a month of work should be *timely* remunerated. It should be settled on or before the last weekday of the month.

Paying People Better for Work – on Time

There is much wasted time, from lunch-time, to the time employees spend trying to figure out a way to get home because they have *fulizad*, and now they are tapped out; they have asked all and sundry for bus-fare and it is only but the 22nd day of the month, and the bank account they have has not been visited for more than 5 years (or at least since MPESA passed the threshold of possible dysfunction and became the main banking system).

Much time is wasted in traffic in the morning, in the evening going home, and one contends that at least, Kenya ought to try to see if staggering work schedules, arrival and departure time, and lunch time, firms would operate more efficiently and profitably. Then again, maybe we have never been the kind to do things the easy way when there is a hard way.

More broadly, it is important to sensitize Kenya into a culture of *better work conditions*. The strike cycle of the Kenyan professional life is both predictable and distressful. First, lecturers strike, then university staff and somewhere in there, students strike. Then the medical services take up the mantle, and we see strikes among doctors, nurses and orderlies. After that, teachers threaten their own strike, and the cycle restarts again.

Most of these occupations are employed by the government, and one would like to think that the government has funds (they do collect taxes, develop budgets and even allocate monies to the different spending categories). It is therefore impossibly confounding, why there are always strikes, and the amount of time wasted on song and dance and twigs, where the government *still* pays for the time spent striking.

Tragically, strikes have contributed to negative outcomes for students, pupils and patients seeking medical care, including critical services such as dialysis. While one sympathizes with the clear need for better pay, the notion of people dying because there is a strike and the employer refuses, or slows down pay, is unconscionable. It is most surprising that legal action has not been taken to sue the government for negligence that caused innocent patients' deaths.

And the strikes do cause deaths: one of the most recent, 2021 strikes saw a number of patients shuffling from one hospital to another as medical staff went on strike. While we fully expect the Hippocratic Oath to apply to medical services employers, there should never be a situation in which governments – county or national – fail to negotiate, or pay salaries, and lead to Kenyan patients dying as a result.

A further issue related to strikes, pay and remuneration, and future solutions to these perennial crises presents. Often, when a new government comes into power, the Legislature's first business is to carve out special funding for themselves – whether it is the interest-free car grants, loans to purchase houses, state-provided health insurance of the highest quality (unlike NHIF), their lifetime pensions, a retirement 'sum' of Kshs. 100,000 a month (not sure why), or the other perks that give the *distinct impression that the country has money.*

When medical orderlies go on strike, asking for a Kshs. 5,000, or 10,000 increase, it is exceedingly difficult to argue that a government that just gave MPs a Kshs. 5 million interest-free car grant is unable to afford such small increases. It becomes a cyclical hostage-taking spree. There is a solution no one wants to hear of, but one that works quite well: any benefits for legislators should take effect the earliest after the current parliament, so as to remove incentive to increase one's pay.

Negotiating work conditions so that strikes, especially within the critical services are exceptions if not exceedingly rare events should be the reality. After all, we have avoided any instances of the uniformed services going on strike. But we should also consider strategies to remunerate individuals well, with increases and benefits that reflect their contribution to this collective that is Kenya.

We should also look into other ways in which employers can improve their employees' overall happiness and productivity. Besides paying better wages, paying on time, staggering work hours and lunch hours, companies that invest in support systems such as possibly, day-care services, travel vouchers if not transport services, providing employees paid vacations and not just to Mombasa among other things can vastly improve overall productivity, contributions to companies and economy.

Is Lunch Time – Wasted time?

Gabriel Omollo captured the essence of lunchtime in Kenya in his famous song *Lunchtime.* Nothing is probably as confounding as the practice that was – probably – inherited from the British all those years ago. Every 12 o'clock sharp, like clockwork, on the clock, (most) working Kenyans stream out of their offices for lunch, several tens of thousands of them.

These hardworking Kenyans dutifully flock into cafes, restaurants and hotels, to religious services and a healthy many, to the available public squares (or concrete spaces) to wait out the lunch hour, ready to do it again tomorrow. Some, the pay not enough to procure lunch, take advantage of the rather interesting 'street food concerns', which sell all kind knickknacks and home-made foods consisting of eggs, sausages and related food products sometimes spiced up by the dust of the streets.

Eateries are especially busy during that one (lunch) hour, but it has always confounded one whether having staggered lunch hours would be a good thing or not. Having *most* of the workers flood the streets at the same hour decidedly creates another rush, but staggering them would cause less of a crush, servers would have fewer people to serve simultaneously, and therefore, likely serve more efficiently, while patrons would not be in the mad rush one often sees, returning to the office.

There is no evidence that all body metabolisms work the same way, and therefore, that everyone needs to take lunch at exactly 12-1. Government cannot make this policy, but these are some of the issues that Kenyan companies should look into, with a view to treating employees as partners, work, rather than time-bound entities. However, lunch is done now, one suspects that the current system wastes a lot of time.

Traffic Lights, Violations and Traffic Police

This may have more to do with our discipline as Kenyan drivers than with anything else, particularly how we manage travel during the critical hours of the morning and afternoon. Although the practice is diminishing with the construction of highways, thruways and expressways (ah, but we do put bumps on those), police officers at traffic lights often confuse traffic more than they help, and create a culture of poor driving.

There is a funny, perhaps a tad tragic proposition that traffic lights in Nigeria are 'a suggestion that you could consider maybe slowing down', but in Kenya it is more like, 'why do we have traffic lights and what do they do again?' In some of the advanced jurisdictions from whence we get some of our ideas (at least those on which side of the road to drive on), traffic cameras are able to regulate traffic together with the traffic lights, and thus police officers are only seen when there is an accident or other traffic snarl-up (governor coming through).

With cameras monitoring traffic lights, whenever a driver violates traffic lights, such as going through a red light, or turning right on red when there is a clear prohibition, or even more broadly, violates traffic rules, the camera takes a photo of the license plates. Once captured, the system (and one assumes some humans) generates a violation ticket, and mails it to the address on file at the DMV (of the individual whose vehicle offended, or is registered to). Systems are not perfect, and can have erroneous calibration, but traffic lights tend to lead drivers to better decision-making and driving.

If they don't pay up, eventually it becomes a terrible proposition because collections and even prosecution can occur. With our vehicle registration system, since license plates do not often change, it is possible to make it so costly on a vehicle that it will deter others: say, by charging Kshs. 100 per day for each violation that is unpaid after a grace period of 21 days.

One imagines that most drivers would want to avoid that kind of expense. And in the case of the most notorious offenders, the *matatus,* it is clear that most of them are not owned by the drivers, and it is doubtful that owners will brook paying the fines over their drivers' bad behaviors. One suspects that they would cheerfully pass on the cost to the drivers, thereby reining in some of the bad driving. Indeed, some other possibilities of collecting the money might include being referred to the CRB, or tasking KRA with either intercepting or garnishing tax refunds and other monies to make good on these debts.

These sanctions should extend to *matatus,* trucks and other vehicles on the road, so that driving in Kenya is not always a tryst with destiny in which the odds are not in the obedient driver's favor. There is a place for following the rules of the road, otherwise what kind of country would we have, where one makes up the rules, then doesn't even follow them? Removing the humans between the violation and the punishment, i.e., by using traffic cameras, is probably a much better route than just asking the police officers to apprehend these violations.

Continuing Education as a Matter of Urgency

To reiterate, interruption of schooling should not mean the end of the dreams of millions of Kenyans, of obtaining higher education. The idea that the only way an individual can get to higher education is by completing a linear, 12-year program of primary and secondary school is both unfair, misguided, unrealistic and even self-defeatist.

We want, we should aim to make it so that if students have their education interrupted along the 12-year road, they can resume the education either by distance learning (and now there are platforms, content and providers thereof), or by learning subject-by-subject with an examination within a stipulated period of time so that a certificate of equivalency, for example the General Equivalency Diploma (GED) that is awarded in the US is the ultimate accomplishment. This, of course, is rendered moot by the new CBC curriculum that is bedeviled with issues but a retroactive application of these conditions will ensure that even those who had 'failed' under the old system (which really did fail them) would have opportunity to continue education.

Young persons may have to drop out of school for a variety of reasons. However, later in life, quite a number of people have been able to return to school. This was clearly evident when the 'parallel programs' were introduced. These programs were popular to the point of over-subscription, and one hopes that besides the potential for pay increase and promotion, those undertaking the studies were in fact interested in acquiring an education that could help open up their minds to the oceans of knowledge that they had missed out at some point in their long academic journey. 'Parallel programs' were the first true democratization of the educational space, opening up all manner of opportunity for older adults to acquire education. A well-educated populace, after all, is good public policy.

But beyond this, higher levels of education are better for a country. One presumes that well educated persons are able to debate (even politics) better, that they are more productive, open to new ideas and are a boon for overall social and economic development. There is need for the Ministry of Education to put in place strategies that will allow for the resumption of education without having to return to school, if one is unfortunately forced to stop before they have completed 12 years, or at minimum, stop locking out people on occasion of a slip here or there. That is not the purpose of education.

National Reconciliations and Unresolved Issues

There remains a number of contentious, historical issues that have escaped our collective ability to resolve, much as has been the case with corruption. Kenya's past is littered with unsolved murders of key public figures, unaddressed massacres, abductions and disappearances and other instances that have seen government accused of complicity, including, for example, the Wagalla Massacre. The goal here is not to litigate whether the accusations are accurate; it is to find a way to move forward as a nation.

To heal the nation and move forward in ways that help to strengthen our national unity, it is necessary to confront these issues of the past, otherwise we will continue to have citizens who feel aggrieved but get no justice. And the challenges are not just with the famous; some of the instances have actually occurred in the very recent past. That said, it is crucial for the Ministry of Justice to revisit some of these issues, including, for example, the still 'unsolved' murders of the likes of J.M. Kariuki, Julie Ward, Robert Ouko, etc.

We also need to consider those reports of the 'disappearing Kenyans.' The numbers of these keep rising, and while it is often suspected that such abductions might be related to criminality, there is a presumption of innocence until proven guilty. That is the Kenya we live in. We are not a banana republic, we are not Argentina with its *desaparecidos,* and there isn't some ghost or ghoul snatching people off the streets.

Government and its agents should especially never be accused of nefarious activities towards their citizens.

Illicit Drugs: A National Drug Policy

No nation is immune from the scourge of illicit drugs, and Kenya has not been the exception to this. Increasing interactions between Kenya and the outside, frustrations among the youth, certain measures of wealth and the nefarious actions of allegedly well-connected individuals has seen a proliferation of ever more serious and harmful illicit drugs. In especially high schools and college campuses, drugs are becoming a major menace and negatively impacting individuals, including their productivity.

There is a future, almost certain downside to drugs: addiction. We have already seen what addiction can do especially to our youth but across the spectrum. A challenge that has been occasioned by 'street boys' and the petty crimes that they commit on occasion are an indication of what embers exist in our society, and if allowed to continue, that would be Kenya on a large scale. Additionally, the growth in their numbers and threat they pose to the security of specific areas of the city, making them less attractive for business.

But even more importantly, drugs can lead to health issues, to a 'wasted generation' of drug addicts, and to expensive rehabilitation needs, for a country where even sufficient food can be a challenge. There is need for the government to urgently confront the issue of drugs in a systematic way. These include especially convening a drug task force that will address the various issues associated with drugs, and will include developing a robust national drug policy.

It will also entail increasing the training with an eye toward interdiction and prosecution of drug dealers (but also major users), and providing more resources to ensure that those in need of rehabilitation access those services, as well as follow–up opportunities such as funding for the 12-step program and other non–punitive, non–incarceration responses that work. It is the pretender who suggests that drugs are not an issue: they are, the issues are here, they are a menace and present a growing problem. It is urgent that we decide on a strategy to address the issue.

Africanizing Kenya

It is entirely possible that there exists a lake in the United Kingdom, named after Jomo Kenyatta, i.e., (Kenyatta Lake – although one seriously doubts that there is). Since independence, Kenya, as with most other African countries that found themselves, at some point or other, colonized by European powers, has progressively taken steps to rid itself of European references to its infrastructure – roads, streets, buildings, parks, even entire regions. These include, for example, Government House, Grogan Road and Lake Rudolf. Why Lake Victoria has still not been officially named after Obote, Kenyatta, Nyerere or even Obama is still a mystery worthy of Sherlock Holmes' expertise.

We ought to sit together with our East African brethren and agree to eradicate a name, and all other names, that remind us so much of colonialism and its associated evil. And some of the names do remind us of that dark past: my mother was held in those British *gulags* Caroline Elkins wrote about. The benefit of retaining the names cannot be greater than the need to remove the names and be proud of our - stuff. Or we could demand that The Thames be named after, say, Nelson Mandela or some other African person of consequence, such as the most recently departed Archbishop Desmond Tutu.

Merely Mild Annoyances: Zebra Crossings

In all the years of traversing mist cities in Kenya, I have never been fortunate enough to see a zebra cross the street. Maybe it's just my luck. The Britishness we inherited causes us to think that Zebra Crossing is a thing. We should definitely change this into 'pedestrian crossing' for one is likely to see lots of pedestrians, and likely no zebras.

And while we are at it, nothing makes British English inherently more superior than other forms of English. Cultural diversity requires that we recognize other versions of common languages, including English, perhaps to include pidgin and our more local hybridized variety, Sheng. We ought to stop being so righteous about British English; after all, are we really going to defend our oppressors, even though at this point one might wonder how the sun never set on the empire? Perhaps not.

Kenyans' self-reliance vs. Nanny State

Even as we expect government to improve its conduct across different issues and endeavors, and to provide the conditions that are necessary to allow citizens to thrive, we should also perhaps take a moment to review our expectations of government, as Kenyans. It is most interesting to watch TV news especially in instances where there is a natural calamity. Kenyans have adopted an attitude of helplessness. Some of this is understandable, because some challenges are natural phenomena, and are often beyond the capacity of any one person to solve. But even as we deal with such issues, we have often taken our quest for help from the government entirely too far.

Most news interviews with citizens who have been affected seem to end with the now-predictable entreaty: 'tunaomba serikali itusaidie.' It is not clear, sometimes, how we as citizens expect the government to help us, particularly in some of those events that are nobody's fault, or even are a result of the poor choices that we occasionally and inevitably make. But also, we should encourage citizens to consider such programs as private property insurance, to pay for such damages.

This tradition of expectation is often influenced by election campaigns that feature monetary giveaways, the *harambee* activities and ideas of being subject to the shared destiny that often leads us down these expectations. Unfortunately, we seem to have created a 'nanny state' and our collective expectations are that the government will 'help us,' however that understanding of help manifests in real life.

We ought to encourage citizens to recognize that the government is not the end-all, be-all. That there are things that we as citizens should expect the government to do, and others, not. On the other hand, we need to cherish our ability to help others, but to also recognize that government cannot solve every problem that we have; neither should it be its responsibility to do so. Government should also stop being the overbearing, make-believe solution for all citizens' challenges.

The Great License Plate Fraud

Perhaps even greater than Goldenberg or Anglo-leasing, the greatest fraud ever conspired against the Kenyan people is in the registration of motor vehicles. Overwhelmingly, Kenyans are sold on the fraud that the license plate – or the number plate – denotes how new a car is. Nothing could be further from the truth, and it is worth considering how we can save generations of Kenyans from spending hard earned money for lemons and really older vehicles. And for those who are familiar with vehicle registration, one can be certain that this is as frustrating as anything one can imagine.

There are several things that ultimately determine the letters and numbers on the number plate that is placed on any one car. They include a) whether it was imported as a chassis (those, which become trucks and buses and minibuses, are the truly new vehicles – then fabricated in Kenya), b) when it was manufactured; for example, most cars made after 2020, unless they are basic models, have driver assist and all manner of cameras or are even self-driving, c) when the vehicle was imported into Kenya, d) when the vehicle was actually registered and e) whether it is a first instance, or re-registration.

Vehicles imported as a chassis and built by the likes of LSHS (Labh Singh Harnam Singh) or KCI (Kenya Coach Industries) are usually new, and once built, are generally registered. Those are new vehicles that get completed as bus, coach, minibus, truck and commercial vehicles. While there are other cars that are imported as new (for example, most government vehicles), your regular Box, Toyota Premio, Fielder, Passo and the like are mostly imported used (so technically, 'new' to Kenya). There is a distinction here: is the vehicle imported after it has been used, or never used? This class of vehicles that are sold in Kenya after some use locally are thus 'third hand', not 'new,' unless one is using the nuanced version.

Here, the challenge begins. Imagine you import a vehicle from Japan. It was manufactured in 2014 and used for 2 years in Japan, then sold. It is sold and exported to Kenya (that's how you might purchase it). But, the ship was delayed forever (think Evergreen stuck in the Suez), sat in a lot in Mombasa, then a dealership, then wasn't purchased for a year. This vehicle, once sold and registered, would take on the *newest* number plate. This does not mean that it is new in any manner of speaking.

There are thus two critical variables to focus on, when purchasing a vehicle. The first is the year of manufacture – here, newer cars are more likely to have newer technology than older cars, including, for example, rear-view cameras. The second is the total distance the vehicle has traveled before you take it on. Some people drive their vehicles like there is no tomorrow.

It is not unusual to find a vehicle manufactured in 2020 having 120,000 km and one manufactured in 2014 having only 6,000 km. One presumes that fewer kilometers is a good thing; cars break by being driven a lot, parts grind, accidents happen, and the wear and tear is definitely much more. Less driving = more perfect car. The third item one might look into is whether the vehicle has been used in Kenya; Kenya's roads are rough, so they do take a toll on a vehicle. When these criteria are satisfied, then you are in the market for a vehicle.

Here is a perfect and practical example. A neighbor bought 3 cars, one was a KCW xxxx (2012 manufacture, 120,000 km), a KDC xxxx (2014 year of manufacture, 6,000 km original) and a KDD xxxx (2014 manufacture, 80,000 km). If one were to ask for a recommendation for selection (assume all the cars are the same brand), one would be well served to take the KDC xxxx, because even though KDD is newer, both were made in the same year, but KDD has traveled more miles, and is therefore likely to break down sooner than the KDC.

Yet most Kenyans would think that the KDD is the newer vehicle, notwithstanding they were made the same year but registered slightly apart. This is how Kenyans get conned into purchasing vehicles for high prices even though the year of manufacture might be super-old but it was registered most recently. Not most Kenyans concern themselves with all of these issues, and so those who sell and register vehicles regularly pick up on this and sell the 'registration', so that the vehicle looks more new than it is, and is sold for a fortune.

We propose to completely overhaul the vehicle registration system, and further, to decentralize it as part of the devolution. For starters, each county should have an NTSA office that will do the vehicle registration in that county, so that people can choose where to register vehicles. These should be at the Huduma Center, together with the KRA offices which are generally to be found in each county. Second, we will overhaul the number plate system. Although we may shun re-registration of current vehicles, every new vehicle after August (after implementation) will use the new system.

Each vehicle would begin with K (Kenya), the County number (3-digit, e.g., K001), a hyphen, then 2-digit year of manufacture (e.g., '14 for 2014) and a letter and/or combination of 3-4 random numbers. While the exact math on that numbers or letters following the first 5 items may be later decided, a vehicle manufactured in 2019, imported and registered in Mombasa would have a license plate that looks something like this: K001-19-M0001. A vehicle manufactured in 2000 in the same county might have a plate like K001-00-M9900. In an instant, that license plate gives you a lot of information, whether you are a citizen or a police officer.

The objective of this campaign and the subsequent movement is to foster *A Better Kenya.* While government cannot be the nanny to all and sundry, it is an obligation so that even when government does things that are punitive to citizens (vehicle registration is completely a government affair), these can be regulated and corrected. For the government to know and continue with the perpetuation of the great grift is just wrong, and it is something that can be corrected. It is time to stop deceiving, or at any rate, participating in the deception of Kenyans by using the number plate and vehicle registration system.

National Identification Cards for Under-18

How do you identify and find a lost/missing/trafficked/exploited 8-year old? Apparently, there is no sure way to do so. It is not the case that many Kenyan children are born in hospitals or other health centers, and home-births are still prevalent. In addition, not everyone is Christian, and so children are not always baptized. Some children only speak their mother-tongue, and except for those in urban areas, rarely learn English or Swahili until they enter school.

The safety and security of such children is endured by their parents, guardians and others who have legal responsibility over and in such a child's life. But what would happen if there was an incident in which such a child went missing? How would they be identified, especially since they are quite likely to tell you that their name is "Jane wa Mum," and since they carry no other identifier, and clearly might have no birth certificate or phone number on them?

Most adults today got their birth certificates long after they were born (mine was at 25 years of age). We do unequivocally blame the British for the failure to ensure registration of births was done on a regular basis and more births done in hospital, we are more than half a century into our own management of our affairs. Yet, it would seem that we have adopted a posture of not wanting to know, deciding not to know or identify in a systematic way, or simply ignoring the need to identify who our children are, at least until they are about to enter school. This is dangerous, for there are 5-7 years during which our children are 'unofficially' known, and even with the 'Nyumba Kumi,' it is impossible to know all the children in an area.

There is a simple fix to this, and it is not based on the newer National Education Management Information System (NEMIS)[45] and its Unique Personal Identifier (UPI)[46] for each pupil. While NEMIS was an inspired idea, it fails to account for the pre-CBC entry, or school entry, period. Children need an ID that identifies them, like they have in many other countries. The comparison might not be apt, but good ideas are good ideas notwithstanding where they originate.

The US' system of registration of persons is creative: in some states, at birth, the baby's toes are 'fingerprinted' and imprinted on the back of the original birth certificate, issued by the medical facility of birth. Within a few months after birth, they are issued with a Social Security Number (SSN) that rarely, if ever, changes through life. At any point thereafter, a parent or guardian can obtain a State ID for the child, with the appropriate documentation such as a birth certificate.

Clearly, while the baby is too young to carry it, one assumes that when a toddler, or any child below 18, they have some form of official identification, particularly when they are younger and not able to articulate their origins or parents. However, this could also replace all the myriads of different identification numbers and often, documents a Kenyan has to carry through life.

The Kenyan ID card, for majority of its use, serves as a form of identification needed to complete various actions and activities: employment, registering to vote, obtaining a passport for self and children, registering a phone, land or property, death certificates and for a number of other official business matters. While a child, or youth, may not need to do any of these things, the basic function of the Identity Card is –

identification. While we are at it, perhaps Safaricom might find another way to record individuals' details when they withdraw money. Those books are often left on counters, the ID number and name are right there, and this cannot possibly be good data protection practices, considering what country we live in.

It is time that Parliament put in place the legislation that will facilitate for anyone below the age of 18 to obtain an authorized, recognized form of ID, at no cost to Kenyans. As a parent, I am sure I would be most appreciative if, in the event of an ELE where my child went missing, I would want for others to be able to identify them. In the worst case scenario, this would allow them to return the child to the place where they can then be reunited with the parents.

A second proposal is to distinguish the 'child ID' from the regular ID, e.g., by printing the holder's details in portrait rather than landscape. It would render the ID unusable for anything other than identification, ruling out such things as employment or purchase of items such as liquor. Thus, these conditions would safeguard the traditional ID and its lawful functions, and render the 'under-18' ID unusable in capacities other than identifying the child.

Voter Registration and Electoral Integrity
We are in the process of preparing for the 2022 General Elections. Between the present and the 9th of August, there will be many millions of young Kenyans who will turn 18. The IEBC cannot be in the business of disenfranchising Kenyans, by only registering voters whenever they fell like it.

It is our objective to ensure that the IEBC look into having a full-time presence in each of the counties, at the Huduma Centers or at the County headquarters or some other easily accessible location. After all, voting may be a party affair, but it is also a Kenyan affair. Just as we pay taxes and therefore find the KRA offices across the country, IEBC offices should be too. We should be doing everything to ensure that voter registration is an ongoing affair, all year through, not just monthlong sporadic occurrence as we do now. There should, in fact, be provisions for registration of new voters on voting day, with voting taking part provisionally if one's ID can be verified.

Non-registration cannot be a reason to deny Kenyans a right that they get to exercise only on one occasion every five years except in the instance of a by-election. And when non-registration occurs, it is the case that the fault lies not with the new citizen, but with the agencies that are tasked with ensuring proper voter registration, and more broadly, the government. In addition, we are cognizant that the IEBC is aware of the timelines of the elections and of new citizens who will be of age, but they cannot get identification.

There is need to plan ahead, and to ensure that there are no gaps in registration and participation in elections by Kenyans, especially younger ones who come of age within the time-frame when they should be participating in the most sacred of all undertakings: voting. Nothing could be more important for a newly-minted Kenyan than to participate in one of the most meaningful activities of the republic. Turning 18 in the in-between period between registrations is not a reason to exclude younger Kenyans from voting.

Kenyans, Diaspora and Voting

To say that Kenyans who live in the Diaspora are important to the overall infrastructure of the nation, and that they deserve, in fact should be, part of the electoral system, is an understatement. One can appreciate the challenges of registering voters and ensuring a credible, well-organized election by those in the Diaspora, but on the other hand, the fact that Diaspora Kenyans do not have the occasion to vote is almost unfathomable.

Some of the requirements that IEBC puts in place can be quite the challenge. Even for those who live near Kenyan embassies and consulates can experience significant challenges in attempting to vote, especially if such voting is to be done at the consulate or embassy. A distance of 200 miles, or 320 kilometers, can sound like it's really close, but to have to go that far, while one could reasonably mail a ballot, can be a hardship. One is moved to consider whether electoral authorities in the countries where Kenyans live might be encouraged to receive ballots – probably a tall order, but voting has to be more efficient – in fact, simply done, for it is a right of citizenship.

Even if the IEBC does not go this route, it is imperative that IEBC put in place strategies, or at minimum, trust the systems that are in place to facilitate Kenyans' activities in the countries in which they are, short of physically presenting themselves at the embassy or consulate, to potentially vote. If Kenyans are able to send their passports to the embassy or consulate and they arrive safe, there is no reason why the same cannot be done with ballots. Of course IEBC would have an official at each of the embassies, but the potential downsides on that or the security of the ballot pale in comparison with the great cost of not voting.

Kenyans in the Diaspora should not be excluded from the electoral process just because of where they live, particularly given how much they contribute to the welfare of Kenyans and the amount of money they send back as remittances. But money is not the issue: the issue is the participation of Kenyans in systems and practices assured of them by the constitution. It is time to ensure that all Kenyans of the majority age can vote, whether or not they live in Kenya or in the Diaspora.

A Peaceful, Prosperous and Better Kenya

Every election is a challenge (it does not have to be), but the notion that we cannot conduct free and fair elections ought to be in our collective past. The past few by-elections have demonstrated that we can, indeed, campaign, vote, report results, accept the win (or defeat) and move on to build a better nation, together. This coming election's stakes are almost impossibly high, but with such stakes, the probability of situations being unstable in the country increases.

The end of the second term of the current president means that there is no incumbent, and therefore, stakes are especially high, but also, considering political schisms and non-support of the current DP by the president makes the situation even more precarious. But stakes being high do not mean that we should forget that at the end of the election, we still have children to educate, bills to pay, loans to repay, *chamas* to contribute to, weddings, funerals, economic activity to carry on with and a country to generally run. In fact, for most of us, elections 2022 will not have any significant impact on how we lived life before the election compared with life after the election.

The 2007 General Election hopefully taught us lifelong lessons, lessons we should have learnt by observing others and not needing to actually tempt the gods of conflict. The lesson is that peace is fragile, conflict is expensive, disagreements can and do burst into the open and cause low-intensity war and that putting a broken egg back together is almost impossible, so we should not break the egg in the first place. We know now, if we didn't, that neighbors can turn to enemies, that friends can do the same. We have become even more cognizant that our peace must be guarded jealously, never sacrificed at the altar of elections, no matter how important we deem them to be.

The post-election years also procured change, some that we had been seeking for near eternity, including, ultimately, the 2010 Constitution. But like the old adage about ignorance says, 'if education is expensive, try ignorance,' We do not need to tempt the gods of war again and again, at every election, just because certain leaders lost or thought the election was, to quote a certain American president, 'stolen from us.'

Servant leaders must always remember that there is no one with the divine right to rule, or to be president of Kenya. The late George Saitoti's 2002 concession that "there comes a time when the nation is bigger than an individual"[47] was half true: as far as politics and political leadership, there is never a time when an individual is bigger than a nation. That is our lesson.

It is incumbent upon all those who seek political office to concede that though they, their friends and families, neighbors and supporters might imagine that they have the best ideas on the planet, even galaxy, there will always be people who see things differently, who disagree, people who think that there is a better path than that which they propose.

We ought to see, and learn from most of our neighbors, how conflict over political disagreements go (badly). Further, we have to always remember that earth is not large enough for those whom the ICC targets, and that even heads of states can become the accused and suffer the humiliation of being hauled off to the ICC to answer for alleged crimes. This, the 2022 General Election is the most important election yet, but it is just that: an election, one in a line of many elections we have had, and will continue to have. We would be ill-advised to 'burn destroy the village to save it.'[48] And in truth, on the day after the elections, we will still have to carry out our tasks as we did before the election. We would like to continue to have a great space, and country, to carry out those actions that life has bestowed on us.

This is our path to *A Better Kenya*.

Epilogue

 C3🙰C3🙰C3🙰

The 2022 General Election will be held later this year, on 9th August, *ceteris paribus.* We are a little over 7 months away from the day Kenyans go to the polls and elect leaders who will guide the country through its next five years, and into what is anticipated to be the accomplishment of Agenda 2030. There are many challenges that face Kenyans, even now, before, during and after the elections.

Government is not always the solution to citizens' challenges. In fact, sometimes, government is the problem (as this is being written, the Sudanese government has been breaking up protest, with at least four deaths recorded). But government does not have to be the, or a problem. By individual citizens giving up the private right to exact their brand of justice and violence, government can and does provide the necessary conditions for citizens to pursue independent and group actions that improve peoples' overall and general welfare.

Rhetoric during election often becomes heated, as we have already begun to see with politicians' pronouncements. This is not always very useful – in fact, it is rarely useful. We tend to let our passions to get the best of us, and often, when our candidate loses, we take to the streets and seek to change the outcome thereof. We must always pledge ourselves to the idea that the voter has the power to give us a job, or deny us the opportunity based on the strength – or weakness – of our arguments. Heated rhetoric and incitement is absolutely the wrong direction to go in, and we must be committed to a peaceful, prosperous Kenya, no matter what the outcome of the election, whether we win, our candidates win, or if our opposition wins.

It is therefore necessary that all candidates commit to a) violence-free elections; b) bribery-free elections, c) free and fair elections; d) accepting the results of the election as the expression of the will of Kenyans, and e) to subject themselves to the formal judicial and/or arbitration processes that are in place, so that the challenges can be dealt with, without loss of life. We, and especially this candidate, commits to all of the above, and will accept the results of the elections as the true will of the people of Kenya.

Leaders must especially commit to peaceful elections, to deterring any possible violence in their name or the name of their political campaigns, shun hate speech in any form (written, audio, social media) and to sensitize their followers and supporters to absolutely commit to keeping Kenya peaceful after the election. On our part, we are now committing (as we have always been) to peaceful elections and to a Kenya that will be better in every possible perspective.

References

______ "Regional Analysis of Youth Demographics: Kenya," Briefing Note – UK Government, December 2021, https://assets.publishing.service.gov.uk/media/5af9544740f0b622d7cc6e58/Kenya_briefing_note__Regional_Analysis_of_Youth_Demographics_.pdf

African Union, "African Summit on HIV/AIDS, Tuberculosis and other Related Infectious Diseases. *African Union – Abuja Declaration*, OAU/SPS/ABUJA/3, 24-27 April 2001, URL: https://au.int/sites/default/files/pages/32894-file-2001-abuja-declaration.pdf

Baraza, Lawrence. "75 percent of Kenya's population is aged below 35 years." *Metropol TV*, February 24, 2020, https://metropoltv.co.ke/2020/02/24/75-percent-of-kenyas-population-is-aged-below-35-years/

Central Bank of Kenya (CBK). "Annual GDP – Kenya." *Republic of Kenya – The Central Bank of Kenya.* December 2021. URL: https://www.centralbank.go.ke/annual-gdp/

Central Bank of Kenya (CBK). "Diaspora Remittances." *Central Bank of Kenya*, 2021, URL: https://www.centralbank.go.ke/diaspora-remittances/

Government of Kenya. "Flagship Programmes: NHIF Expansion." President's Delivery Unit, December 2021. URL: https://www.delivery.go.ke/flagship/nhif

The Greenbelt Movement. "Who We Are." *The Greenbelt Movement.* December 2021. https://www.greenbeltmovement.org/

Human Capital. "Personnel Suitability Guidance Position Sensitivity and Public Trust Risk Level Determinations Q&A." *USGS – Human Capital.* December 20, 2021, https://www.usgs.gov/human-capital/personnel-suitability-guidance-position-sensitivity-and-public-trust-risk-level-0

IFAD. "Remittance flows to Kenya defy the odds during the COVID-19 pandemic." *International Fund for Agricultural Development (IFAD).* Press release No.: IFAD/23/2021. 25 May 2021, https://www.ifad.org/en/web/latest/-/remittance-flows-to-kenya-defy-the-odds-during-the-covid-19-pandemic

ILO. "Kenya: Inua Jamii Senior Citizens' Scheme." *ILO Social Protection Department.* May 2019. https://www.developmentpathways.co.uk/wp-content/uploads/2019/05/Inua-Jamii-Country-Brief-1.pdf

Ingraham, Christopher. "There are more guns than people in the United States, according to a new study of global firearm ownership." *The Washington Post – Economic Policy Analysis.* June 19, 2018, https://www.washingtonpost.com/news/wonk/wp/2018/06/19/there-are-more-guns-than-people-in-the-united-states-according-to-a-new-study-of-global-firearm-ownership/

Kenya Data Portal. "Kenya Population by Demographics." *Kenya National Bureau of Statistics.* December 2021, https://kenya.opendataforafrica.org/lpdtibb/kenya-population-by-age-groups

KHCR. "Consortium Applauds Court Judgement Declaring Huduma Cards Illegal; Calls for Further Reforms. *Kenya Human Rights Commission – Press Release,* 18 October 2021, https://www.khrc.or.ke/2015-03-04-10-37-01/press-releases/754-consortium-applauds-court-judgement-declaring-huduma-cards-illegal-calls-for-further-reforms.html

KLRC. "Preamble." *The Kenya Law Reform Commission* 2021, https://www.klrc.go.ke/index.php/constitution-of-kenya/107-preamble

Kuguru, Peter N. *Trailblazer: Breaking Through in Kenya.* Nairobi: Transafrica Press, 2008

Lambert, Linda. "Overview: Leading in Challenging Contexts." In *Women Leading Education across the Continents: Overcoming the Barriers.* Edited by Elizabeth C. Reilly and Quirin J. Bauer. Lanham: Rowman & Littlefield, 2015

Maxon, Robert M. "Economic and Social Change Since 1966." In *Historical Studies and Social Change in Western Kenya: Essays in Memory of Professor Gideon S. Were.* Edited by William Robert Ochieng'. Nairobi: East African Educational Publishers, 2002

Migration Data Portal. "Migration and Development – Remittances." *Migration Data Portal.* 3rd June 2021, https://www.migrationdataportal.org/themes/remittances

Ministry of Education. "The National Education Management Information System (NEMIS)." *Ministry of Education. Republic of Kenya.* December 2021. URL: http://nemis.education.go.ke/

Ministry of Environment and Forestry. "Submission of Kenya's Updated National Determined Contribution [NDC]". *Office of the Cabinet Secretary. Ministry of Environment and Forestry. Republic of Kenya.* 24th December, 2021. URL: https://www4.unfccc.int/sites/ndcstaging/PublishedDocuments/Kenya%20First/Kenya%27s%20First%20%20NDC%20(updated%20version).pdf

Ministry of ICT, Office of the Data Protection Commissioner. "Strategic Plan FY 2021-2023: Promoting personal data protection by design." *Ministry of ICT*, October 2021,

https://ict.go.ke/wp-content/uploads/2021/10/ODPC-
Draft-Strategic-Plan_v2.5-20211021.pdf

Ministry of Public Service, Youth and Gender. "Kenya Youth
Development Policy 2019." *Ministry of Public Service,
Youth and Gender, State Department for Youth*, 2020.
https://youth.go.ke/wp-content/uploads/2020/11/Kenya-
Youth-Development-Policy-2019-Popular-version.pdf

Mpungu, Pauline. "Despite pioneering ban. Kenya is drowning
in single-use plastic." Al Jazeera. 4 Dec 2020.
https://www.aljazeera.com/economy/2020/12/4/despite-
pioneering-ban-kenya-is-drowning-in-single-use-plastic

Mukii, Irene. "1.1 Million Kenyans to Get Kshs 8,000 Through
Inua Jamii – Who Qualifies." *Kenyans.Co.Ke.* 18 February
2021, https://www.kenyans.co.ke/news/62368-over-1m-
kenyans-get-ksh-8000-pm-who-qualifies

The U.S. National Archives. "Declaration of Independence: A
Transcription." *The US National Archives – America's
Founding Documents*. Page last reviewed October 7, 2021.
https://www.archives.gov/founding-docs/declaration-
transcript

National Council for Law Reporting (Library), "The Data
Protection Act, No. 24 of 2019," *The Kenya Gazette
Supplement, Acts, 2019*. November 11th, 2019,
http://kenyalaw.org/kl/fileadmin/pdfdownloads/Acts/201
9/TheDataProtectionAct__No24of2019.pdf

Ndungu, Tonny. "Out of 47.6 million Kenyans, 35.7 million
are under the age of 35." *Citizen Digital*, February 21,
2020. https://citizen.digital/news/out-of-47-6-million-
kenyans-35-7-million-are-under-the-age-of-35-323822/

Njuguna, David and Pepela Wanjala, "A Case for Increasing
Public Investments in Health – Raising Public
Commitments to Kenya's Health Sector," *Ministry of*

Health, Policy Brief, 2021, https://www.health.go.ke/wp-content/uploads/2019/01/Healthcare-financing-Policy-Brief.pdf

The Nobel Prize. "The Nobel Peace Prize for 2004." *The Nobel Prize*. 2004. https://www.nobelprize.org/prizes/peace/2004/press-release/

Otieno, Otieno, "Ruto may have attracted more trouble at Bomas," Nation Media Group, Sunday, November 01, 2020, https://nation.africa/kenya/blogs-opinion/opinion/ruto-may-have-attracted-more-trouble-at-bomas-2727382

Owino, Anthony. "NEMIS: How to Register & Track Learners' Performance in Kenya." *Kenyans.co.ke*. 28 June 2019. https://www.kenyans.co.ke/news/41166-nemis-how-register-track-learners-performance-kenya

Research Consulting. "Assessing the needs of the research system in Kenya." *Report of the SRIA Programme*. October 2019, https://assets.publishing.service.gov.uk/media/5ef4acb5d3bf7f7145b21a22/NA_report_Kenya__Dec_2019_Heart_.pdf

Rossiter, Caleb Stewart. *The Weathermen On Trial: A Bombshell Story About Bringing the War*. New York: Algora Publishing, 2019

United Nations. "UN Documentation: Environment." *UN Dag Hammarskjold Library*. December 2021. https://research.un.org/en/docs/environment/conferences

United Nations. "Youth 2030: Working with and for Young People." *United Nations Youth Strategy – United Nations*, 2019. https://www.un.org/youthenvoy/wp-content/uploads/2018/09/18-00080_UN-Youth-Strategy_Web.pdf

Usher, Anthony. *The Emancipators from Lincoln to Obama.* New York: Page Publishing, 2015

The World Factbook. "Kenya." The World Factbook, Updated December 14th, 2021. https://www.cia.gov/the-world-factbook/countries/kenya/#people-and-society

YEDP. "Youth Enterprise Development Fund Strategic Plan, 2020/21 – 2023/24." *The Youth Enterprise Development Fund,* December 2021. https://www.youthfund.go.ke/wp-content/uploads/2021/03/YEDF-STRATEGIC-PLAN-2020-TO-2024.pdf

Notes

[1] KLRC, "Preamble," The Kenya Law Reform Commission (KLRC), 2021, https://www.klrc.go.ke/index.php/constitution-of-kenya/107-preamble

[2] National Archives, "Declaration of Independence: A Transcription,{" The US National Archives - America's Founding Documents, Page last reviewed October 7, 2021. https://www.archives.gov/founding-docs/declaration-transcript

[3] Robert M. Maxon, "Economic and Social Change Since 1966," In William Robert Ochieng', Ed., *Historical Studies and Social Change in Western Kenya: Essays in Memory of Professor Gideon S. Were,* (Nairobi: East African Educational Publishers, 2002)

[4] Anthony Usher, *The Emancipators from Lincoln to Obama,* (New York: Page Publishing, 2015)

[5] IPPRA, "Kenya's Public Debt with the COVID-19 Pandemic," Kenya Institute of Public Policy Research and Analysis, June 4, 2021, https://kippra.or.ke/kenyas-public-debt-with-the-covid-19-pandemic/

[6] CEIC, "Kenya Government Debt: % of GDP - 2009 - 2020," CEIC: Global Economic Data, Indicators, Charts & Forecasts, URL: https://www.ceicdata.com/en/indicator/kenya/government-debt--of-nominal-GDP

[7] IPPRA, "Kenya's Public Debt with the COVID-19 Pandemic," 2021

[8] David Herbling, "Kenya Resumes China Debt Repayment With $761 Million," *Bloomberg – Economics,* July 31, 2021, https://www.bloomberg.com/news/articles/2021-07-31/kenya-resumes-

china-debt-repayment-with-761-million-remittance
9 Herbling, "Kenya Resumes China Debt Repayment With $761 Million," 2021
10 CEIC, "Kenya Government Debt: % of GDP - 2009 - 2020," 2021
11 World Bank, "Kenya Economic Update: Transforming Agricultural Productivity to Achieve Food Security for All," April 8th, 2019, *The World Bank – Where we Work*, https://www.worldbank.org/en/country/kenya/publication/kenya-economic-update-transforming-agricultural-productivity-to-achieve-food-security-for-all
12 CBK, "Diaspora Remittances," Central Bank of Kenya, 2021, URL: https://www.centralbank.go.ke/diaspora-remittances/
13 The World Bank, "Access to electricity (% of population) - Kenya," *The World Bank Group*, December 2021, https://data.worldbank.org/indicator/EG.ELC.ACCS.ZS?locations=KE
14 Government of Kenya, *Flagship Programmes: NHIF Expansion*, President's Delivery Unit, December 2021, URL: https://www.delivery.go.ke/flagship/nhif
15 Njuguna David and Pepela Wanjala, "A Case for Increasing Public Investments in Health: Raising Public Commitments to Kenya's Health Sector," Ministry of Health, Policy Brief, 2021, https://www.health.go.ke/wp-content/uploads/2019/01/Healthcare-financing-Policy-Brief.pdf pp. 1
16 ILO, "Kenya: Inua Jamii Senior Citizens' Scheme," *ILO Social Protection Department*, May 2019, https://www.developmentpathways.co.uk/wp-content/uploads/2019/05/Inua-Jamii-Country-Brief-1.pdf and Irene Mukii, "1.1 Million Kenyans to Get Kshs 8,000 Through Inua Jamii – Who Qualifies," Kenyans.Co.Ke, 18 February 2021, https://www.kenyans.co.ke/news/62368-over-1m-kenyans-get-ksh-8000-pm-who-qualifies
17 African Union, "African Summit on HIV/AIDS, Tuberculosis and Other Related Infectious Diseases," *African Union - Abuja Declaration*, OAU/SPS/ABUJA/3, 24-27 April 2001, URL: https://au.int/sites/default/files/pages/32894-file-2001-abuja-declaration.pdf
18 Linda Lambert, "Overview: Leading in Challenging Contexts," In Elizabeth C. Reilly and Quirin J. Bauer, Eds., *Women Leading Education across the Continents: Overcoming the Barriers*, (Lanham: Rowman & Littlefield, 2015), 123
19 D. Odondi. "Kenya Population." OCHR, 2019. https://www.ohchr.org/Documents/Issues/Youth/D_Odondi_Kenya.pd

<u>f</u>

[20] Tonny Ndungu, "Out of 47.6 million Kenyans, 35.7 million are under the age of 35," *Citizen Digital,* February 21, 2020, https://citizen.digital/news/out-of-47-6-million-kenyans-35-7-million-are-under-the-age-of-35-323822/

[21] Lawrence Baraza, "75 percent of Kenya's population is aged below 35 years," *Metropol TV*, February 24, 2020, https://metropoltv.co.ke/2020/02/24/75-percent-of-kenyas-population-is-aged-below-35-years/

[22] Kenya Data Portal, "Kenya Population by Demographics," *Kenya National Bureau of Statistics*, December 2021, https://kenya.opendataforafrica.org/lpdtibb/kenya-population-by-age-groups

[23] The World Factbook, "Kenya," The World Factbook, Updated December 14th, 2021, https://www.cia.gov/the-world-factbook/countries/kenya/#people-and-society

[24] United Nations, "Youth 2030: Working with and for Young People," *United Nations Youth Strategy – United Nations*, 2019 https://www.un.org/youthenvoy/wp-content/uploads/2018/09/18-00080_UN-Youth-Strategy_Web.pdf

[25] ____ "Regional Analysis of Youth Demographics: Kenya," *Briefing Note – UK Government*, December 2021, https://assets.publishing.service.gov.uk/media/5af9544740f0b622d7cc6e58/Kenya_briefing_note__Regional_Analysis_of_Youth_Demographics_.pdf

[26] YEDP, "Youth Enterprise Development Fund Strategic Plan, 2020/21 – 2023/24," *The Youth Enterprise Development Fund,* December 2021, https://www.youthfund.go.ke/wp-content/uploads/2021/03/YEDF-STRATEGIC-PLAN-2020-TO-2024.pdf

[27] Ministry of Public Service, Youth and Gender, "Kenya Youth Development Policy 2019," *Ministry of Public Service, Youth and Gender, State Department for Youth*, 2020, https://youth.go.ke/wp-content/uploads/2020/11/Kenya-Youth-Development-Policy-2019-Popular-version.pdf pp. 3.

[28] Ministry of Public Service, "Kenya Youth Development Policy 2019," (2020), 3

[29] Migration Data Portal, "Migration and Development - Remittances," *Migration Data Portal*, 3rd June 2021, https://www.migrationdataportal.org/themes/remittances

[30] IFAD, "Remittance flows to Kenya defy the odds during the COVID-19 pandemic," *International Fund for Agricultural Development* (IFAD), Press release No.: IFAD/23/2021, 25 May 2021,

https://www.ifad.org/en/web/latest/-/remittance-flows-to-kenya-defy-the-odds-during-the-covid-19-pandemic

31 According to *Statista,* https://www.wipo.int/ipstats/en/statistics/country_profile/profile.jsp?code=KE. Comparatively, 391,103 patents were granted in the US in 2019 alone

32 Research Consulting, "Assessing the needs of the research system in Kenya," *Report of the SRIA Programme*, October 2019, https://assets.publishing.service.gov.uk/media/5ef4acb5d3bf7f7145b21a22/NA_report_Kenya__Dec_2019_Heart_.pdf

33 Ministry of ICT, Office of the Data Protection Commissioner, "Strategic Plan FY 2021-2023: Promoting personal data protection by design," Ministry of ICT, October 2021, https://ict.go.ke/wp-content/uploads/2021/10/ODPC-Draft-Strategic-Plan_v2.5-20211021.pdf

34 National Council for Law Reporting (Library), "The Data Protection Act, No. 24 of 2019," The Kenya Gazette Supplement, Acts, 2019, November 11th, 2019, http://kenyalaw.org/kl/fileadmin/pdfdownloads/Acts/2019/TheDataProtectionAct__No24of2019.pdf (pp. 3)

35 KHCR, "Consortium Applauds Court Judgment Declaring Huduma Cards Illegal; Calls for Further Reforms, Kenya Human Rights Commission - Press Release 18 October 2021, https://www.khrc.or.ke/2015-03-04-10-37-01/press-releases/754-consortium-applauds-court-judgement-declaring-huduma-cards-illegal-calls-for-further-reforms.html

36 Christopher Ingraham, "There are more guns than people in the United States, according to a new study of global firearm ownership," *The Washington Post – Economic Policy Analysis*, June 19, 2018, https://www.washingtonpost.com/news/wonk/wp/2018/06/19/there-are-more-guns-than-people-in-the-united-states-according-to-a-new-study-of-global-firearm-ownership/

37 Human Capital, "Personnel Suitability Guidance Position Sensitivity and Public Trust Risk Level Determinations Q&A," USGS - Human Capital, December 20, 2021, https://www.usgs.gov/human-capital/personnel-suitability-guidance-position-sensitivity-and-public-trust-risk-level-0

38 Ministry of Environment and Forestry, "Submission of Kenya's Updated National Determined Contribution [NDC]", Office of the Cabinet Secretary, Ministry of Environment and Forestry, Republic of Kenya. 24th December, 2020. URL: https://www4.unfccc.int/sites/ndcstaging/PublishedDocuments/Kenya%

20First/Kenya%27s%20First%20%20NDC%20(updated%20version).pdf

[39] Ministry of Environment and Forestry, "Submission of…" (2020).

[40] Central Bank of Kenya (CBK), "Annual GDP - Kenya," December 2021, URL: https://www.centralbank.go.ke/annual-gdp/

[41] United Nations, "UN Documentation: Environment," UN Dag Hammarskjold Library, December 2021, https://research.un.org/en/docs/environment/conferences

[42] The Greenbelt Movement, "Who We Are," The Greenbelt Movement, December 2021, https://www.greenbeltmovement.org/

[43] The Nobel Prize, "The Nobel Peace Prize for 2004," The Nobel Prize, 2004, https://www.nobelprize.org/prizes/peace/2004/press-release/

[44] Pauline Mpungu, "Despite pioneering ban, Kenya is drowning in single-use plastic," Al Jazeera, 4 Dec 2020, https://www.aljazeera.com/economy/2020/12/4/despite-pioneering-ban-kenya-is-drowning-in-single-use-plastic

[45] Ministry of Education, "The National Education Management Information System (NEMIS)," Ministry of Education, Republic of Kenya, December 2021, URL: http://nemis.education.go.ke/

[46] Anthony Owino, "NEMIS: How to Register & Track Learners' Performance in Kenya," Kenyans.co.ke, 28 June 2019, https://www.kenyans.co.ke/news/41166-nemis-how-register-track-learners-performance-kenya

[47] Peter N. Kuguru, *Trailblazer: Breaking Through in Kenya*, (Nairobi: Transafrica Press, 2008), 167

[48] Caleb Stewart Rossiter, *The Weathermen On Trial: A Bombshell Story About Bringing the War*, (New York: Algora Publishing, 2019)